Knowsley

Memories of
Rugby League Football Club

By Andrew Quirke

Next match at Knowsley Road (Photo: Chris Gill)

LONDON LEAGUE PUBLICATIONS Ltd.

Knowsley Road

Memories of St Helens Rugby League Football Club

A CIP catalogue record for this book is available from the British Library.

First published in Great Britain in August 2001 by:
London League Publications Ltd.
P.O. Box 10441, London E14 0SB

ISBN: 1-903659-04-3

Cover design by: Stephen McCarthy Graphic Design
                          46, Clarence Road London N15 5BB

Layout: Peter Lush

Printed and bound by: Catford Print Centre, PO Box 563, Catford,
                          London SE6 4PY

For Mum - the unofficial secretary to the author!

Foreword

The memories are still vivid when I reminisce about my times at St Helens - truly the most enjoyable experience I've had in my Rugby League career. I remember how the team would warm-up either on the Knowsley Road pitch or outside and not a person to be seen! Then, as we made our way out of the dressing sheds to start the game, the roar and chanting of the fans was awe-inspiring. You had to play well, one couldn't afford not to, otherwise the disappointment of losing would affect the whole team.

The high esteem the people of St Helens bestowed on the Saints players was incredible. I felt the enormous responsibility that comes with such praise and the friendship of people involved with the club from the coaching staff, players, committee members and their families made it so much easier. To our benevolent friends and supporters, thanks for making my wife Debbie and I feel so welcomed. I hope to return one day.

Knowsley Road no more! Sad, it still touches the heart of all followers of St Helens including me. Times are changing, however memories are everlasting. That's what is important, I remember my first game for Saints and my last at Knowsley Road against our old foe Wigan – good times!

This book is of memories, memoirs of players and supporters – a special addition to the bookcases of everyone associated with the Saints.

I've witnessed the enthusiasm and passion of the St Helens community personally. I know this book encapsulates that passion and I sincerely hope that all the things that make St Helens a great club and town endure.

Mal Meninga

Mal Meninga played 45 test matches for Australia and was captain of the 1992 team that beat Great Britain in the World Cup Final. He is the only Australian captain to lead two Kangaroo touring teams.

Preface

This book contains recollections from supporters, players and coaches about St Helens RLFC's home ground, Knowsley Road. It recalls some of the memorable matches and players as well as expressing supporters' feelings about the ground as we prepare to bid it farewell. Knowsley Road - the words resonate with the memories of the past 110 years. Heroes and villains have been made there, stars have been born there, trophies have been lifted and missed out on, it has seen any number of star players come and go and coaches depart, yet the ground has remained a constant, a symbol of the club, an immortal. However, the demise of the ground is on the horizon, a ground whose every fibre is soaked in the cheers and boos of the St Helens following, a ground that has seen great tries scored, a ground with turf graced by the legends of the game. Wherever you choose to stand or sit at Knowsley Road, you are following in the footsteps of generations of Saints fans. Walking round the ground, you can imagine all the epic events that have unfolded there, if the ground could talk what stories would it tell? To encapsulate everything that has happened in or around the stadium is beyond this writer but I hope I have captured some of the best.

I would like to apologise to all the great people who aren't featured in this book. All the players, officials, coaches and supporters who have played their unique part in the history of the ground to whom I couldn't talk to or get a story about, this book is for you with my regrets that I couldn't mention you all by name. This book is about people's memories and sometimes players and stories can be missed unintentionally.

To the uninitiated, Knowsley Road looks like an antiquated, ramshackle stadium in need of an overhaul. Parts of the ground haven't been modernised for decades. But, from an emotional point of view, it has been the cathedral where the faithful have congregated to worship the Saints. It has been a focal point for the town. Many of us have grown up around the ground, spent a lot of time there, made lifelong friends there, taken our families there, shared moments of supreme joy and bitter disappointment there. It has been the amphitheatre for gladiators such as Murphy, van Vollenhoven, Killeen, Karalius, Ellaby and Meninga. So, although to the outsider it looks like just an old dinosaur waiting to die, to the faithful, it is so much more...

Andrew Quirke

Acknowledgements

I would like to thank everyone who has helped with this labour of love with special thanks to all those who allowed me to interview them, especially Geoff Pimblett for his invaluable assistance and the Saints Past Players Association. I would also like to thank all those who offered their help, advice, interest or encouragement particularly Peter Lush, Michael O'Hare, Dave Farrar, Paul Wilson, David Burke, Simon Dawson, Gerry Moore, Mike Critchley, Phil Hodgson, Ray French, Kylie Allan, Canberra Raiders RLFC, Mal Meninga, Phil Veivers, Shaun McRae, John Yates, Linda Edwards, Bobbie Goulding, Graham Wilson, Paul Bennett, Tony Bennett, Albert Barker and especially Kevin Gill.

Thanks also to Bernard Platt, Peter Lush, Jack Waring, Jack Coatsworth, John Mantle, Kel Coslett, Kevin, Chris Gill, Mick Gill and Linda Edwards for the photos they graciously let me use.

Andrew Quirke

About the author

Andrew Quirke has been watching St Helens RLFC for over 20 years with his first game being when he was just three years old. During those 20 years, he has commentated for visually-impaired supporters at Saints and spent seven years writing and publishing Saints fanzines. He also used to be the publisher of an independent St Helens RLFC website. He found out recently that Saints were formed at the Fleece Hotel on the 19 November 1873, by coincidence he was also born on the 19 November, just 103 years later!

Interested in Rugby League?

London League Publications are a specialist sports and hobbies publisher. To order our free book-list, write to us at the address below.

Our Rugby League magazine, *Our Game*, is of interest to anyone who follows the game, or is interested in sports history. To order a copy of the latest issue, send a cheque for £2.00 to the address below.

(Cheques to London League Publications Ltd, no credit card orders).
London League Publications Ltd, PO Box 10441, London E14 0SB.

Knowsley Road - then and now

The ground in the 1940s

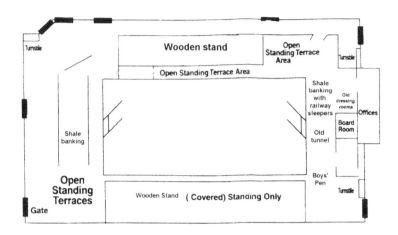

The current ground

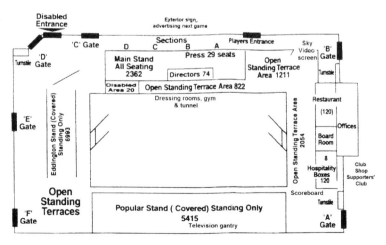

With thanks to the Rugby Football League for permission to use the original diagram of the ground, and to Gerry Moore for advice on the 1940s ground.

Contents

Part 1: Players and coaches

Part 2: Saints Voices

Appendices

The victorious Saints team in the dressing room after the 1999
Super League Grand Final at Old Trafford (Photo: Bernard Platt)

Sean Long kicks for goal against the London Broncos
in front of the Edington end. (Photo: Peter Lush)

Part 1: Players and coaches

Jack Waring
Duggie Greenall
John Dickinson
Glyn Moses
Tom van Vollenhoven
Alex Murphy
Ray French
Kel Coslett
John Mantle
Billy Benyon
Eric Chisnall
Geoff Pimblett
George Nicholls
Harry Pinner
Paul Forber
Phil Veivers
Bobbie Goulding
Shaun McRae
Keiron Cunningham
Chris Joynt
Ian Millward

When embarking on this project, one of the most difficult aspects I had to think about was the players who sadly I would have to leave out of the book. Of course, it would have been impossible to interview every important player or coach throughout the club's history. Deciding who is an 'important' player is also a very subjective matter too, we all have our own opinions on who we think were the 'greats'. As the saying goes, one man's hamburger is another man's steak. It could quite easily be argued that any man who pulled on the famous shirt of St Helens is an important player in his own right.

Imagine if you will that you had to pick the greatest ever Saints XIII. Yours will probably differ from the person who stands next to you at the game, his will contain different players than his wife's selection and her choice of XIII players will be different from that of her son's etc. We all have our favourite players and memories.

Now imagine trying to pick just a small number of the hundreds of players who have turned out for the club in its illustrious history and you will be able to identify with the task I was faced with. Unfortunately it just isn't possible to mention them all.

Some of the players I haven't interviewed could fill a book with their Rugby League exploits on their own. Great names and characters such as Cliff Watson, Vinty Karalius and Tommy Bishop. In later years, players like Neil Holding, Bernard Dwyer and how about the man who enjoyed a career renaissance at Knowsley Road, Kevin Ward? For that matter, what about some of the current players such as the record try scoring Paul Newlove, the loyal clubman and flying winger Anthony Sullivan and the mercurial talent that is Sean Long who is undoubtedly one of the best players in the country.

Then there are some of the Saints legends who have passed away over the years, who no doubt could have contributed their own unique tales of life at Knowsley Road.

What this book does have is at least one player from every decade starting from the 1930s with some of the club's coaches added in as well. Every Saints team or 'era' from the 1930s has a representative within these pages. To those I missed, this book is for you.

Jack Waring

Jack Waring was a Saints centre who made his debut in the 1938-39 season and was tipped to tour Australia with the Great Britain side before the Second World War broke out. In the war, he served his country in the army and also represented England in international Rugby Union, a time when special dispensation was granted to allow Rugby League players to play Rugby Union. Jack also played with Dewsbury and Belle Vue.

I was leading try scorer for Saints in 1939-40 with 18 tries from 28 games. Me and Stan Powell were centres at the time. Later I played centre with Jimmy Stott and I played centre with him a long while. We played the New Zealanders on a Saturday and we all had to go for a massage Sunday morning. We only had one masseur. I was being rubbed down when Oliver Dolan, the coach at the time walked in and said "I feel sorry for you son". I asked him why and he said "You've a brilliant career going west because war's just been declared". Of course, he was right.

I remember at Saints, we had a hooker by the name of Dilorenzo. Dillo used to work at the soap factory and bought washing powders to training and we'd buy them off him. He was a good hooker and the opposition could never get the ball off him. He played in Egypt with me. In the war, we played for England Rugby Union against South Africa and New Zealand. I played fly-half because I'd played stand-off in Rugby League and was used to the position. Dillo was a character and a good friend of mine. By chance, we were brought together to the same base, the sports depot where all the athletes were, in the war. First person I saw when I got there was Dillo.

When I came home from the war I found out that Harold Briscoe, our 16-year-old scrum- half in 1938, had been killed on the last day of the war. He had been blown up. His mother and father were destitute and I tried to get a match organised for them. Unfortunately, Saints said the RFL wouldn't allow it. I had a team willing to play the match, all internationals. They'd have got the biggest gate going for it.

Around the area where I was born in Gladstone Street, you could have had a full team of Rugby League players including internationals. There was Duggie Greenall at the top of the street, Albert Johnson, Abe Terry and so on.

Knowsley Road was always a smashing ground to play on. Having said that, the best ground for playing rugby on in this town was St Helens Recs at City Road. It's a pity Recs had to finish. The derbies we had with Recs were fabulous games, there was never a lot between the two sides. Some wives would be glad if Recs won as real Saints supporters would be going home too upset to eat if they'd got beat by Recs and the wives wouldn't have to make the tea. They were that keen about the game. When you had the derby with Recs on a Saturday, the pubs would be full on the Friday night with people talking about the forthcoming game.

I used to love playing against Wigan. I got on well with all the Wigan players like Ken Gee and Joe Egan.

I've got a good story about Ken Gee that Martin Lawrence, another Wigan player who I got on well with, told me. They were on the Australian tour with Great Britain. A scrum packed down 20 metres from the Australian line, the ball was fed in and came out the other side. The ref said: "Wheel round England, wheel round, wheel round." One of the British players shouted out: "Shut your effin mouth for God's sake." The referee broke them up and asked: "Who said that?" The answer came back "Ken Gee Sir, Ken Gee" and Ken was sat up in the stands watching the game. When they told him later, he laughed his head off.

The best try I ever scored was at Knowsley Road against Swinton. We were on our own 25 and we had a scrum. I said to Harold Briscoe, the scrum-half, I'm going round the blind side so give it us quick. I went round, I sold the dummy, I went up the middle, Harry Pimblett, one of our lads, followed me. I came to Palin, the Swinton full-back, I went straight up to him, gave a little motion to pass the ball, he took the dummy and I ran another 30 yards and went in under the sticks at the Edington end. Palin came to me after the match and said: "You made a right fool of me."

I guested for Dewsbury and the Saints supporters were unhappy that I went because I was well-liked. The reason I guested for Dewsbury was because Saints were paying 30 shillings, £1.50 for a win, 35 bob for a draw and a pound for a loss. Eddie Waring, Dewsbury manager at the time, sent for me and a few others from Saints including Jack Bradbury. The money there was nine pound, win, lose or draw. That was a good start plus we got expenses. Our expenses were about half a crown and we got three quid out of them. I was in my pomp at this time and Dewsbury were signing up all the better players. They had Jim Sullivan at full-back, the finest goalkicker in the world and he was on £12 a match. They're on about Andy Farrell kicking 200 goals, Jim Sullivan would have kicked 300. We finished up a good team, we had a good side.

Jack Waring on his debut for St Helens
(Photo courtesy Jack Waring)

The teams for St Helens versus Belle Vue 7 April 1947, Jack Waring playing for Belle Vue

I never thought Saints would move. I don't agree with Knowsley Road going. It's been there that long and everybody's got used to it. I think it's a big mistake.

I still bump into some of the players I played with and against at various dinners they have for past players.

I still go watching Saints, I particularly like the Wigan, Leeds and Castleford games. I rate Keiron Cunningham very highly. He gives you 80 minutes every week. Tommy Martyn has got a rugby brain.

I played against Iestyn Harris's grandfather who played centre for Oldham. He didn't like being tackled. Everytime I knocked him down he used to curse me. If I was playing against Iestyn Harris, as the ball met him I'd meet him and I'd knock him down.

It's a different game today. Rugby League for me was the finest game in the world when we played it. Today, they've done away with the scrum-half and the open side prop used to help the hooker get the ball, they don't need that now with the way they feed the scrums. The referee could put the ball in the scrums today. The full-back role has changed as well, you used to get great kicking duels which was brilliant to watch. Also, the full-back letting the ball bounce into touch and not picking it up, that's not rugby. Martin Ryan, the Wigan full-back would have had a field day today. You notice today that a full back will catch the ball and run into the defence and accept the tackle. Martin Ryan would think nothing of beating four or five men.

If Murdoch hadn't have stepped in with his money, a lot of the clubs would have gone to the wall. In my opinion, it's these players' agents who have a lot to answer for. Taking players on and demanding this, demanding that. Rugby League clubs can't afford the contracts they are paying. I think we should stop all these Aussies coming over, they're only has-beens and our public is paying for them. Look at Renouf at Wigan. He was a belting centre four seasons ago, best in the world. Once you've lost that yard of pace in the three-quarter line and you're not big enough to play in the pack, you're finished. It happened to Gus Risman, brilliant player, who I played with at Dewsbury. When you lose that yard, you've finished.

People come up to me in town sometimes and ask me: "Can you tell me about such a game in 1939?" I say: "What are you on about? I can't even tell you what I've had for breakfast!"

Duggie Greenall

Duggie is one of the real characters in the club's history and pound-for-pound one of the hardest too. He signed for Saints as a 17-year-old in 1944 and played at centre, captaining St Helens and England. He had a unique and devastating crash tackling style and played in 489 games for Saints before leaving the club. He was also known for singing the Al Jolson number Mammy.

I first came to Saints with the Air Training Corps. Harry Cook was involved with the cadets and also involved with Saints. During the war, on some days to get a team they would shout in the stand: "Have we got a hooker here?" just before the match to make up the team with members of the crowd. To help make the team, some of the cadets would play and that's how I got started.

What did Saints in the 1940s was the war. Saints had a lot of young international players who went to the war. Players like Jack Waring, an excellent centre, and Harold Briscoe, the great scrum-half.

The farmers used to put cows on the Saints' pitch during the summer to keep the grass short. So, when you were training on the pitch you had to keep an eye out for cow pats. There was also a slight incline on the pitch when I first played there so there was an advantage playing towards Fletcher's farm. Mind you, that was dependent on the smell coming from the pigs on the farm which the opposition wouldn't know about but we did. It was never a bad pitch though and there were a lot worse around in those days.

We used to do our sprint training behind the stand where the railway lines used to be. Just after the war, the blackout was still on and there were no lights anywhere. The coach to smoke a cigarette so we used to sprint towards that.

In the late 1940s they levelled the ground and put topsoil on it. We came off it after the first match looking as black as the ace of spades. Then they laid this special seed on top and that's been the ground ever since. I don't know what they've done with it in the past few years but that turf we played on lasted for years and years.

The goalposts were never padded in those days, I was going for a tackle once and I missed the fella and I hit the bloody goalpost. The spike from the top of the post came off and fell towards me and missed me by inches. From that day on, they started padding the posts.

Knowsley Road had one big bath for both teams, there wasn't that much water in it, they had that bath for years. There was a lot of talking in that bath especially with the opposition.

Saints couldn't give us jerseys at one point. It wasn't that they were poor, it's just that they didn't have enough clothing coupons. So the Griffin pub in College Street had a collection of clothing coupons and got us a kit of white with a red band. It turned out when they washed it the red would run pink. Then we had an orange kit with strips of brown on it. We had an all-blue kit. We had kits made of flour bags which weren't comfortable as you can probably imagine.

Duggie Greenall (Photo: Andrew Quirke)

8

The main controversy in my career was the "*Mammy*" business. I had orthopaedic felt under my jersey to protect an elbow problem I had. It wasn't a plaster cast as the Aussies later claimed. They thought that when the Saints supporters shouted to me 'Give 'em Mammy Duggie' they were referring to a plaster cast on my arm that I was secretly using to lay the opposition out with.

When I went to Australia with Great Britain in 1954 I ended up on the front of their papers with one of the captions stating "the bad man arrives today". I wouldn't mind but I was only ten stone six pounds, I had lost a stone on the very long plane journey. When I arrived in Sydney there were more cameras waiting for me than there had been for Frank Sinatra the week before.

The only *Mammy* worth talking about was the rendition I sang on the Town Hall steps to thousands of supporters when we came back from Wembley in 1953.

I used to take my share from opposition players but I would always be ready to have my turn with them. My tackling style was like a snake. I would get you in my sights, line you up and pounce like a snake in the grass, that would be it, you would be down.

Van Vollenhoven was amazing, he wasn't a wingman who would barge into you, he had tremendous pace and you couldn't get hold of him. The 1958-59 season when I was centre to him he scored 60 odd tries and I got at least 30. Over 90 tries from one side of the field. Voll was a great wingman

Then you had Steve Llewellyn, Voll never did anything Steve didn't do. I would pass the ball to him and he would take it while diving towards the line, that's how he scored a lot of his tries. Someone once asked me: "What's the longest dive he has done for a try?" and I told them "From the 25 yard line and he flew over the crossbar so the ref gave him an extra two points."

We've had some great wingers at the club and it just depends what generation you are from. The older ones say "Alf Ellaby was the best, you'll never beat him". Alf was great. McCormick came and you'd hear "good 'un but not as good as Ellaby". Then van Vollenhoven came over, I remember his first match at Saints. I was trying to give him inside balls and everything and he couldn't keep hold of the ball. However, he scored the last try when he got the ball ten yards from his own line and he was just away, no-one could get near him and he scored under the posts. Alf Ellaby's legend died that day in many ways at Saints. It's been all van Vollenhoven ever since. Karalius was the loose forward, he would give me the ball and I'd feed it to Tom with no room to work in on the touchline but he'd be away. The full-back would have no chance.

I always liked beating Wigan. Even in the bad days in the 1940s when we were struggling we would always give them a good game. We would very rarely beat them but we would give them tough matches.

Then in the early 1950s, one Good Friday, we didn't just beat them, we slaughtered them and we never looked back after that match. We won trophy upon trophy and I think Wigan only beat us once in the 1950s. In 1952-53, we never lost an away match, scored more points than anyone else, broke all kinds of records and were getting a very high average gate.

Jim Sullivan [Saints coach from 1952 to 1959] had a hell of a lot to do with our success. Saints had always signed the best players but couldn't get a winning team. Without Jim Sullivan, Saints wouldn't be what they are today.

I had my ups and downs with him though. I remember once he made me travelling reserve for an away match and on the way back I asked for my transfer. It ended up in a showdown with the board and Sullivan said to them: "You might as well keep Greenall and I'll go". The board would have done but I said to him: "Don't pack it in Jim".

Before Sullivan came to the club, Stan McCormick was in the A team looking like he was finished. When Sullivan arrived, McCormick would be training every morning at half seven and not only got back into the first team he got back into the international scene. He was a good player, before he came to Saints I'd never seen his type of tries scored. I'd seen plenty scored against us but none for us.

There were a lot of good players around like Ken Gee and Joe Egan at Wigan as well as Don Gullick for us, he was a hard man and a good player.

To get to Wembley is a great thing but to lose there against Huddersfield in 1953 was very disappointing. We had gone there too sure we were going to win. When we returned to St Helens though, you wouldn't have thought we had lost, there was thousands there to meet us with Church Street packed with people. I sang *Mammy* for them and I said: "We'll bring the Championship Cup back for you" and we did do. We played Huddersfield the week after at Knowsley Road and slaughtered them.

When we won the cup in 1956 there were even people in Lime Street and London Road stood round waiting for us when we came back from London to Liverpool on the way to St Helens. Coming down Prescot Road was amazing, there were thousands of people.

Wherever I went throughout the town I would be asked: "what's the team on Saturday Duggie?" and so on. We used to get thousands to watch us train at the ground. We used to be playing tick rugby and with the crowd on it was just like a proper match.

I went to the Millennium dinner of the Past Players at Huddersfield [June 2000] recently. When Malcolm Lord announced my name to go on the stage, everyone stood up and there was booing, cheering, clapping, everything. The name Duggie Greenall is still well-known outside the town in other clubs, not just St Helens. I got a good benefit off the club. I think it's a shame that they're leaving the ground, there's a lot of tradition there.

John Dickinson

'Todder', as he is commonly known by St Helens supporters, played for the club between 1950 and 1958. He made 158 appearances and scored 42 tries. He played in every back position for the first team before the age of 18 and eventually settled at stand-off.

My first game at Knowsley Road was against Huddersfield in the days when they had a good side. I don't think I was even 17 when I played and I remember in the second half I threw a long ball out and they intercepted and scored. I couldn't believe it. I didn't do too bad apart from that though. The reports on me were pretty good.

The pitch at Knowsley Road wasn't as good as it is in modern times. For me, Saints is now one of the best pitches in the league. I remember talking to one of the groundsmen at Wigan once and he told me that Knowsley Road has been so good over the years that when it does go bad they don't know how to treat it.

The most memorable game I played in at Knowsley Road is probably when we played Huddersfield the week after they beat us at Wembley in 1953. We murdered them that day, we run them ragged.

The Saints players I played with who stand out for me are obviously Alan Prescott, Duggie Greenall and Vinty Karalius.

As a coach, Jim Sullivan was the best. I'm not only talking about footballing ability but the way he treated players also. I read these articles today where it says the player didn't know they'd been dropped until they read it in the paper. We used to train on a Tuesday and Thursday in them days. They used to put the team sheets in shop windows. I'll always remember, I was an apprentice cutter at Pilkington Glass, I used to walk through Pocket Nook down Park Road on my way home. The chippie down there used to have the team sheets up on a Tuesday night. I always used to have a look, making sure I was on. This particular Tuesday night, I'm walking home and I see on the sheet that I'm in the A team. By the time I got to Knowsley Road for training, the first man who met me was Jim Sullivan. He told me why, I'd had a couple of bad games, he told me to get out there with the A team on Saturday and pull my finger out and if everything went according to plan I'd be back the following week. Sure enough, I was. He was a gentleman. The players used to say anything they wanted to him as a laugh but they respected him. Glyn Moses, Duggie and fellas like that used to take the 'Michael' out of him but I tell you what, they'd have died for him. He was brilliant.

We beat the Aussies in 1952 and 1956 at Knowsley Road and I scored in both games. At the time, we were expected to beat them. We were a good side. The Aussies were as good as they are today in my opinion but the English game seems to have gone backwards.

There is one word that no-one seems to bother about today and that is dedication. There was no ale after the matches with us. We had tea and biscuits after the game and that was it. I can tell you my typical week when I was playing at Knowsley Road. We used to play on a Saturday in those days. Me and Vinty used to go to Warrington dog track on a Saturday night. There were no cars, I mean Duggie had a battered old thing and so did Alan Prescott. Apart from that, everyone was on buses. I would get the bus from St Helens at about 7pm on a Saturday night after playing in the afternoon. Vinty would do the same coming from Widnes. We'd spend the night on the dog track. We'd get the bus back and I'd get off in St Helens. It used to be 'Co-op' dancing in those days for the young ones. I'd go there for half an hour and then get the last bus home. Sunday night, we always went the pictures. Monday night was usually a night in, Tuesday night was training. Sometimes Wednesday night was a training night if you went to the local gym. I mean, Vinty used to train every night and if he thought he could do anything to improve himself like make himself bigger or get more pace then he would do it. Thursday was a training night and Friday you didn't go out because you were playing the next day. Now, they can't get to the bar quick enough. That's the difference today. The Aussies are dedicated. I can tell you in the past few years when the Aussies have played at Knowsley Road, straight after the game they've gone back to the hotel to prepare for the next match.

I remember playing in one of the later matches of my time at Knowsley Road and we played Swinton when they had a good side. Reg Senior was playing for them that day, he later came to Saints. He wasn't a bad lad and he was a hard lad as well. Him and Duggie were marking each other and had been having a bit of a do. Both sets of forwards were in the scrum and as stand-off I was watching to see whether we would get the ball as you had to fight for it in those days. I suddenly heard Duggie singing *Mammy* to Reg. I could hear this "I'll walk a million miles" being belted out by Duggie. Reg was getting really angry over this, the hairs were standing up on the back of his neck, and he was shaking his fist and saying: "I'll effin' give you *Mammy*."

I still go to watch Saints today, I hardly ever miss a match. I'm particularly impressed by Keiron Cunningham, the half-backs are quite good, and Newlove on his day is as good as anything.

Knowsley Road has been like a monument to me really. You've got to go on with the times though I suppose. If they can get all the funding and grants for a new ground which they can't get for the old one, well then, maybe we've got to move.

Glyn Moses

Glyn played full-back in the 1950s after joining the club on Christmas Day 1952. He had previously played for Salford and Cardiff. He had left Salford and returned home to South Wales. The Rugby Football League had given him permission to play for the struggling Cardiff side, but he had to stop when Salford demanded a transfer fee. Jim Sullivan brought him back to Rugby League and agreed a transfer fee with Salford. He was a part of the victorious Saints Challenge Cup winning team in 1956 as well as lifting numerous other trophies with the side during those years. He made 258 appearances for the club, and also played for Great Britain.

The main reason I decided to join Saints in 1952 was that I was missing my rugby. Also, Saints was a club on the way up then. Previously, I was on Salford's books and they stopped me playing in Wales. I played with Cardiff Rugby League for a spell.

I thought very early on that Knowsley Road was fantastic. I stayed at the Fleece Hotel for a fortnight which wasn't too bad. I joined the club in December 1952 and my first losing money only came at Wembley in 1953. It was a cracking start and we had some good seasons after that.

I remember that in my debut I was playing centre with Jimmy Stott who was one of the older players at the time.

I think that due to the success we had the crowd was always behind you. Every time I played there, the St Helens crowd were fantastic.

I always found that Knowsley Road was like a homely ground. The stands were quite close so you weren't too far away from the crowd. If you went into touch, the crowd was there with only the wall between you. You could talk to some of them if you wanted to. A very compact ground and a good ground too. Excellent drying out ground, you never get many matches postponed at Knowsley Road due to the conditions. The pitch was always in good nick.

As soon as you came through the tunnel at Knowsley Road, that was it, the noise of the crowd hit you, particularly in the big games.

One of the highlights of my time at Saints was bringing the Challenge Cup back to the town in 1956, that was fantastic. It was a great occasion and everybody celebrated for weeks.

One match at Knowsley Road that stands out for me is the week after we lost to Huddersfield at Wembley, we played them at home in the Championship play-off and we beat them convincingly. Of, course beating the Aussies at the ground was good in 1956, we gave them a good hiding. It doesn't happen much these days but I suppose the Aussies have come on a bit.

Amongst my team-mates at Saints were stars like van Vollenhoven and Murphy. Then you had the tireless Alan Prescott. You also had the workers who perhaps didn't get the recognition as much as others did, such as Steve Lllewelyn, a steady wing man.

Among the opposing players who stand out for me there is obviously Billy Boston. There was Dave Valentine, the loose-forward from Huddersfield who was a good player and of course Brian Bevan from Warrington. Bevan was a cracking winger. At full-back I would often come into contact with the likes of Bevan, although sometimes I didn't as I missed him!

It was a bit sad when I ended my career. I had hurt my leg on the 1958 tour of Australia. It never came right. I must give credit to the club, they kept picking me but I knew it wasn't right. I saw a few specialists but it never came right for me. It was sad because I felt I could have gone on for another two or maybe three seasons. I'd had a good run though.

Glyn Moses (photo: Peter Lush)

Out of the current crop, I think Tommy Martyn is an outstanding footballer. He makes the odd mistake as we all do, the reason he makes them though is because he gets so involved. He's one of the good all round players of modern Rugby League.

I occasionally see some players of my era at reunions. The likes of Alex Murphy, Eric Ashton, Frank Carlton and Austin Rhodes. I see quite a few of them.

Tom van Vollenhoven

Voll is a legend in St Helens and Rugby League as a whole. He made his Saints debut in 1957 and stayed at the club for 11 years, making a total of 409 appearances and scoring 392 tries for the club. This included the 1958-59 season where Tom scored an incredible 62 tries in 44 games. A former South African Rugby Union international Tom, twice a Challenge Cup winner with the club, is held in the highest esteem by his fellow players and remembered in awe by St Helens supporters. He is the scorer of some of the greatest tries ever seen and on 25 November 2000 was inducted into the Rugby League Hall of Fame at half-time during the World Cup Final.

I was first approached to join Rugby League by Warrington before St Helens or Wigan got involved. That was in 1956 and I wasn't interested at that stage. Then in 1957 I was approached by Wigan firstly, then St Helens. Obviously, I had to make up my mind which club I would go to. I sent each club a telegram at the same time stating that whichever club offered me the most money would be the offer I would take. St Helens did that and they beat Wigan by a few hours. I kept my word and signed for Saints. [Both clubs had offered an identical signing-on fee.]

My first game at Knowsley Road was against Leeds on 26 October, 1957. All I can remember is that the ball was over our try line and instead of kicking it dead I hesitated and Leeds scored. Then in the last minute I received the ball from Ray Price and all I had to do was run it to the tryline to score my first try for Saints.

During my time at St Helens, I had a record written about me *The Vollenhoven Calypso*, that was quite a nice thing to have.

I feel more at home in St Helens than sometimes I feel in my home town. St Helens has been really good to me. I'm very fond of the place and all the people there. It's lovely to go back there. Whenever I have come back to St Helens and been greeted by the present day supporters, it's something you must experience to believe it. You don't whether to cry or laugh. It's one hell of an experience to receive such a welcome. The St Helens crowd has always been good to me. They've always looked after me.

I liked to play and I liked to score tries, fortunately I did quite a lot of both. People talk about the Wembley 1961 try but that was a big occasion try. They don't remember the tries I scored against Liverpool City or against Blackpool. Those tries were equally as good but the occasion wasn't as important. I really enjoyed playing at Knowsley Road. I always seemed to score a try in the last minute in games there. That's why the St Helens crowd never went home. It became a sort of ritual for me to score right at the end of a game. I'm sorry that Knowsley Road is going. You mustn't stand in the way of progress. It was home to a lot of us players though. For 11 years, that was my home. I think a lot of St Helens players would feel the same.

"This is one of the memorable days in the history of the Saints. It is the day on which Tommy Voll says good bye to Knowsley Road. Unlike many great players he is doing it while still A GREAT PLAYER.

Also unlike many players of his calibre most of his wonderful feats have been performed off his own bat. But he also had the flair for the great occasion. At Bradford he alone made possible the Championship victory against Hunslet. But at Wembley against Wigan he combined with Ken Large to make the try which will always stand out as Wembley's greatest.

From the game's finest supporters let us offer our token of thanks to the game's greatest artist."

From the St Helens versus Warrington programme 24 April 1968 - Tom van Vollenhoven's last match.

Young Saints fan Amy Heaton wearing Tom van Vollenhoven's training jersey (Photo: Andrew Quirke)

Alex Murphy

Alex Murphy is known to some as the "greatest Saint of them all".
He was part of the glorious Saints side of the 1960s and became the
only St Helens man to captain his home town team to Wembley glory
against the old enemy Wigan in 1966. He played in 320 games for
the club. He left Saints in October 1966 after a dispute and went on
to clubs such as Leigh and Warrington. He returned to Saints in
November 1985 as coach, and left in January 1990.

The most important thing about me going to Knowsley Road for the
first time was that I went there as a kid of 13 or 14. I was invited to
train with St Helens when I was still at school. It was an incredible
experience, you're in junior school one minute and then you're
training with the likes of Duggie Greenall, Frank Carlton, Austin
Rhodes, Vinty Karalius, it's incredible. I was still a little lad and they
were all grown up. You're expected to go out training with fully
grown men.

The first thing is that you're excited to be invited down, it's like
being invited to train with Liverpool or Manchester United. That's
how important it was to me, I wanted to play for St Helens. My dad
took me down, they met me at training and we used to train where
the lottery office is now. The first thing you had to do in training was
sprinting. The first thing I remember was Jim Sullivan putting me
down the track which was about 60 or 70 yards long. He put me there
with Frank Carlton, who is probably one of the fastest wingers in the
club's history, Alec Davies, who was a former schoolboy sprint
champion, and Eric Ledger. Those three were at the finishing line
when I was halfway down.

The place has all kinds of memories for me. The ground is
something that I've seen put together as well as all the changes. The
directors at that time were very good people, the Yearsleys, Joe
Harrison and the Todds. The Yearsley brothers, Frank and Jim, built
the stand. There were tremendous people, such as Lionel Swift who
was one of the directors. There's so many memories, it's not just a
matter of me playing there. The dream was when I signed

professional forms for Saints on my 16th birthday but I'd been down there for two-and-a-half years before that. You get a feeling for the place, it's more than just a rugby ground. I spent a lot of time down there, I was often there a long time before other players turned up for training, it was a different feeling for me.

Joining Saints

I wasn't allowed to sign professionally for anyone until I was 16 but I'd left school at 15. They had to find me somewhere to play for 12 months even though I was training for St Helens. So I went playing for an open age side at St Austins. It came about that the last game, a final against Rivington Institution, was played at St Helens. I was 16 at midnight after that match and had a good game that day. There were scouts there from other clubs, my dad was down there and knew what was going on. Saints knew there was a lot of scouts there and there might have been a lot of temptation. There were scouts from Wigan, Warrington, Leeds, all over the country. St Helens decided to whip me to Joe Harrison's house, who was one of the directors, until midnight. After I had signed, I found out there had been other clubs waiting to talk to me, but I'd signed for St Helens for 80 quid.

At that time, I played rugby with Shaun Edwards's dad Jackie. We were half-backs. He used to play stand-off for Wigan schoolboys while I did the same for St Helens schoolboys. When the pair of us played for Lancashire, I played scrum-half and he played stand-off. We should have signed for Saints together but Jackie ended up going to Warrington.

The pitch at St Helens has always been 100 per cent. We had probably the best ground in Rugby League because we had the best groundsman. Having a groundsman in those days was like having a green keeper looking after a cricket pitch or a bowling green. The groundsman was a fella called Ernie Mills and he knew every blade of grass on that pitch. You had to get permission to go on that pitch. You had no chance of training on there and if you got caught going on there without permission, they'd cut your legs off. There's two people you don't mess with at the rugby club, one is the groundsman and the other is the guy who looks after the kit. They have their own private, divine kingdom. They think that they buy the training kit and the groundsman thinks the pitch is for him. They were great people, they knew their jobs. Ernie Mills was magnificent, he had that pitch like Wembley. It was very rare that a game would be called off at Saints due to bad weather. He could find one of the drains that was blocked on the pitch and fix it without looking at the drawings.

As for people calling me the greatest ever Saint, I don't know what it means. I asked my Dad why are people saying I'm the greatest player they've ever seen, what does it mean? You had people like van Vollenhoven, Dick Huddart, Alan Prescott, Abe Terry, Vinty Karalius, Brian Briggs, Don Vines - all magnificent players. We had a wonderful side. We had all kinds of players who could win you matches. It made me ask Jim Sullivan why were people saying I was the greatest? He said: "Because you can win a match at any time during a game. He said they can cut you off for 60 or 70 minutes but in the 79th minute you'd win the match. You do the same to them and they can't do anything".

Jim Sullivan always explained everything to me. He was like a bloke who's your dad being the coach. Sully had a computer in his head, he could give you so much information. He knew everything about rugby and about what kind of players St Helens wanted. Even now they say Saints are the entertainers and we always have been. Have a look back at how many points the side has scored, how many times they've won the league and how many tries players have scored. There were people like Van Vollenhoven who scored 62 tries in one season and I played as a scrum-half and scored 34. Everyone in the team could score tries and win you matches.

I played the sport because I loved it, I got nothing special, I mean I got a few quid for playing but not a million pounds. I would have played Rugby League for nothing. The money was secondary, yes it was nice when you got winning money. If someone had said: "you're only getting 10 quid today instead of 40", it wouldn't have mattered to me, I'd have just played. You've got to have something inside you that wants to play, yes it's nice to be paid and I don't object to what some of these lads are getting now. They should also realise though that they are very lucky people.

Wembley 1966

On the way to Wembley in 1966 we played Hull KR at Knowsley Road on 4 April and it was a performance we weren't proud of. They had a great night that night with the likes of Harry Poole playing us off the park. We had a full side out, we had no excuses. They were the better side that night no question but I was always told that you play until the referee blows his whistle. Eric Clay was refereeing, I'll never forget it. We were getting beat with time up, in fact they had played three or four minutes injury time and a lot of our spectators had walked off. You know what it's like, people are walking off saying: "Bloody hell they've let us down again, bloody ruined our Wembley trip" and all this.

Anyway I put a high ball up towards their Kellett the full-back. Now I've heard all kinds of stories about what happened. They get better as time goes on, I've heard the ball bounced off the wall and back into my hands and so on. What happened quite simply was that Kellett went to catch the ball and missed it, he fumbled it quite badly. I dropped on it and that was it, we won.

One supporter had already walked off and went into Eccleston Labour Club and he didn't know the score, he didn't realise we had won. He'd booked his trip to Wembley with one of these Wembley clubs and was looking forward to his weekend out. He ordered a pint and the bloke behind the bar says: "What about that bloody lot up there?" referring to the Saints. The guy replied: "What about 'em? They've bloody ruined my Wembley weekend, the bloody shower." The bloke behind the bar said: "What do you mean? They've won". The guy replied: "Hey son, don't take the mickey out of me, it's bad enough, I've just walked off". The barman said: "I'm telling you, Murphy scored in injury time." The guy didn't believe him and decked the bloke behind the bar.

St Helens versus Hull KR - the programme cover from the famous 1966 challenge cup match (Courtesy St Helens RLFC)

It was a game we didn't deserve to win but you need a bit of luck to get you to Wembley. We went on, of course, to win the Cup in style. That Hull KR match was our scare. The games are not only for players, you've got to realise that they're also for supporters. Those supporters were set on their trip to Wembley and they thought we'd let them down. Mind you, two minutes from time we weren't too pleased about things ourselves.

It was magnificent captaining Saints to that 1966 Cup Final win over Wigan, it's something that you dream of. Playing in a game like that against Wigan, a local derby. Rivals of the highest level, no-one wants to lose to Wigan especially if you're from St Helens. That was laid down in stone, you would often be told: "We don't mind what you do all season, just beat Wigan". It was the same for both sides of

23

course. The honour of playing in a final is tremendous, let alone captaining your own side there and leading them out. You can't buy things like that, not with all the money in the world. Wembley is something that a lot of people won't experience, a lot of great players will never go to Wembley. To captain your own side there to a win was a dream come true.

Good times, bad times

As for games at Knowsley Road that stand out, we've had some magnificent games. The games against Australia where we beat them comfortably during the fifties and sixties stand out obviously. What a lot of people don't realise is that the St Helens club is like an institution. The kind of player you sign for St Helens is laid down. 99 per cent of them must be able to play a certain way. Nine times out of 10 they have to have pace, they must have the ability to get on with each other, things like that. Even now, with this generation, people say: "They're letting tries in". The rules at St Helens are quite simple. Jim Sullivan always said to me: "Don't worry about it lads, if they score four tries, you score five". The most important thing at St Helens is winning and the supporters of St Helens never got bored with the type of football that was played. They very rarely got dull or drab games, you'd get the odd bad or boring game but usually, the entertainment football-wise was honestly superb. Some of the games were magnificent, of course I've had some disappointing times.

The most disappointing was when I deliberately ducked out of playing Rugby Union when I went into the RAF to play at Saints. If I had been found out I would have been sent to the other side of Siberia. You wasn't allowed to miss the RAF game against the Army or the Navy. I came up with a cock and bull story to get out of it. Saints played Huddersfield and I played in that instead of playing against the Army at Twickenham. Harry Cook and Basil Lowe, Saints directors, had asked me to get out of the Union match. During the game van Vollenhoven made a break, he had one to beat with me inside him. Peter Ramsden, the Huddersfield player stiff-armed him as Tommy had tried to dummy him. I was so annoyed with Tommy not passing the ball that I leathered Ramsden. Eric Clay sent me off and we lost the match. That was a massive blow to me and I also found out that the RAF had lost. I had to go back to the RAF on the Monday and the words I was met with were basically: "If we don't win this next game against the Navy, you've got big problems". I made sure I played and at Twickenham I didn't let them down and we won.

I was one of the few Rugby League players to ever play at Twickenham. I was allowed to play because as soon as I went into the forces I was classed as an amateur, even though I was a professional.

There was two real hard lads at half-back for Swinton, Parkinson and Cartwright. They were always hard to play against because they thought you were getting a bit too big for your boots. They were always determined to put you down a peg. Playing for Saints and having people telling you were a great player didn't give you any special rights, it made things 10 times harder for you on the field. Playing against the likes of David Bolton, Don Fox, going to Whitehaven then going to Featherstone, playing against Southward at Workington. Then going to Leeds playing against Lewis Jones. These were everlasting great players and they expected you to be like that every week.

Even great players have bad matches though and I was no different from anybody else. Nine times out of 10 though I could handle whatever I was given. I thrived on people telling me that they were better than me. The only way any of them was going to do that was by proving it and not many of them did that. A lot of people used to say: "Oh he's a big headed little bugger" but it was confidence that I had. People might have taken it the wrong way. I never ever thought I was second best to anybody. That's what you've got to do, the only thing with that though is that you've got to go out and prove it. Nine times out of 10 I did that and it was brilliant.

At no time in my life did I ever want to leave Knowsley Road, never. What happened at the time when I was playing there is that people's pride got hurt. You dig in and St Helens as a big club they dug in. Instead of common sense prevailing, sometimes it doesn't.

The longer you are away from the club the harder it is. I was told to stay away from the club and went and trained at City Road and coached Pilks Recs. That's how I got an inkling for coaching. Because I refused to play centre, they wouldn't let me train at the club. It wasn't that I didn't want to play centre, I'd moved from scrum-half after being Great Britain scrum-half to playing stand-off and from being Great Britain stand-off to centre. Played centre and marked Neil Fox and did all right, things like that. My position was scrum-half. I was told later that it was a compliment that I could play so well in different positions.

It hurts your pride though when other people are being brought in. They signed Tommy Bishop in 1966 and I moved to stand-off. I eventually thought if I move any further I'll end up in the stand. I refused to play and if you do that at a big club at St Helens, well it wasn't the best thing St Helens said to me. They knew that stopping me from training was like cutting one of my legs off. If they'd have come back to me the day after and said: "Come back", I would have done. They left it and later on I was told what the truth was. Many years later, I played golf at Grange Park with a director called Sam Hall. He said: "I want to ask you something, you know when we had the bother at Knowsley Road, why did you never ask to see the board of directors?" In those days, Basil Lowe and Harry Cook ran the club. They were the liaison between the directors and the players. I told Sam Hall: "What do you mean? I went to see Mr Cook and Basil Lowe to ask if I could see the board and I was told the board didn't want to speak to me." He replied: "Isn't that funny? We asked Mr Cook if we could see you and we were told you didn't want to speak to us." You can see what was going on, the men who were very important at the club, the secretary and the chairman was keeping the two sides apart. It backfired because it meant I left the club. They wasn't too pleased about that because a lot of things happened after that. Let me put it this way, the hardest decision I ever had to make was to leave St Helens.

Coming back

It was brilliant to come back as coach in 1985. It's another dream come true. You sign for the club, that's your first wish, then you play for the club, then you captain them, then you get picked for your country and I was lucky enough to come back as coach. I just wish I'd have had someone who had money and would let you do the job you want. When I go to a club, two things happen. First, they've no money and secondly they always started telling me how to do the job. But I'd had success at Leigh who were not the best club in the world, yet we'd won many trophies. I went to Warrington who were at the bottom of the league and went on to win a lot of trophies.

Coming back to St Helens was, at first, a dream. At Leigh and Warrington, they allowed me to be a coach, and allowed me to do what I wanted. When I came back to St Helens I had people telling me what to do. I was getting blamed for what was going on so I said: "Look gentlemen, if you want this to happen I think you'd better start picking the team and saying that you're responsible because I'm not taking responsibility for it." It was one of those things.

I still see some of the team I played with although sadly a number of them have passed on. We always had great team spirit at St Helens. There were two things that mattered at the club, one was the supporters. The other was the team spirit which was always second to none.

St Helens is one of the biggest clubs in Rugby League, if not the biggest. It's not just a matter of moving into a lovely new stadium and while I accept that people have to move on, don't forget there's lots of memories in that ground. There's lots of good memories, there's lots of people who've supported St Helens through thick and thin who spent their hard earned money there and died and had their ashes scattered on the ground. There's been a lot of lives been made and died there. It's not a matter of pulling the ground down and forgetting all about it. People have been there for 60 years, all that tradition, then all of a sudden you think: "Knowsley Road, oh it's not there anymore." It's going to very hard. Don't forget there's a lot of Wiganers who've not gone to the new stadium since leaving Central

Park. There'll be a lot of Sintelliners too. I'm not talking about everybody. But it's not the easiest thing in the world. It's not the moving, it's the memories and the emotion. Don't forget that ground has been home to thousands of players and millions of supporters over the years. Knowsley Road is the one thing people know about the town and it's not going to be there. So, yeah it's great to have a new stadium but tradition is a very hard thing to forget. A lot of people will never, ever forget Knowsley Road.

Ray French

Now famous as the BBC's Rugby League commentator, Ray played 201 times for Saints after signing from Rugby Union in 1961. He left the club in 1968 to go to Widnes. Ray was an international in both codes and is now a well-known author of rugby books. As well as his television duties, Ray commentates on Radio Merseyside and is a journalist for the Rugby Leaguer.

I really only played Rugby Union by virtue of going to Cowley Grammar School. In fact, when I started playing Rugby League as a kid in the street up to the age of about 11, I didn't even know Rugby Union existed. When I went to Cowley, they played union and it was a big shock to me as I'd never seen the game. I was a Rugby Union player by accident. I enjoyed Rugby Union though, I still do. I had good years, I played with St Helens, Lancashire, Barbarians, England but always I was Rugby League orientated. Whereas today Rugby Union has a sort of national identity and has big media publicity, in those days it hadn't and in the north of England, it was a very minor sport, as well as being amateur. I always wanted to play Rugby League, I always wanted the challenge. No matter what I did in Rugby Union, no matter how many times I played for England, I still couldn't judge myself as a rugby player until I'd played both codes.

Whether I failed or succeeded at League I had to try it. Finance was also an incentive. I signed for Saints in the August of 1961 for £5,000 tax free which is probably the equivalent today of £250,000. I was at Leeds University for four years and Arthur Clues the great

Australian second rower and Leeds director wanted me to sign for Leeds, in fact they offered me more money than Saints. Oldham, who were a big club at the time, managed by Gus Risman wanted me. I was a St Helens lad though and always wanted to play for my home club. It felt like a natural progression for me to play for Saints. Contemporaries like Peter Harvey and Keith Northey probably had a similar progression.

My first game was in the A team at Knowsley Road. Saints' first team were playing Swinton away who were a very good side in those days. I'd only had one training session and that was a very nervous occasion. Probably, of all the games I've ever played in Union or League, that first training session at Saints was the most nervous occasion in my life. Having watched all my life the likes of Vince Karalius, Dick Huddart, Tom Van Vollenhoven and Alex Murphy, to actually go into that dressing room was quite a humbling experience.

I was almost frightened with regard to how I would go on. How I would cope with these players who I had eulogised over and elevated. I played in that A team game with Frank Barrow who I became firm friends with from that day. My first team debut came on the Tuesday night against Wakefield Trinity, who were one of the top sides of those days, the equivalent of Saints and Wigan today. Saints versus Wakefield was a big game. They had an all-star line up, people like Neil Fox, Alan Skeen the great South African centre, Derek 'Rocky' Turner at loose-forward, Frank Wilkinson at prop, Gerry Round who had been at Leeds University with me and was Great Britain full-back. One of their second rows was Don Vines who had previously played with Saints. In fact, he'd been transferred to Wakefield just weeks previously to me signing. I'd been signed to replace him so there was quite a bit of animosity. There was quite a bit of "I'll show you, you Rugby Union upstart" type of thing. It was a hell of a game. I can remember the first tackle I made was actually on Don Vines. He ran at me deliberately thinking "Rugby Union bloke blah, blah, blah", and I dropped him in the centre of the pitch. He didn't like it and after that it was "hey lads, hey" all the way through the game. We won, but it was one hell of a game with a massive crowd at Knowsley Road.

The crowd received me well as a Rugby Union player coming to Saints. I think me coming from St Helens was also a factor. When Murph left in 1966 after the four cups we won that season, I was captain for 1966-67 and we didn't have the greatest of seasons. Basically, I played in two different eras at Saints in a sense. I went into the 1961 side that had won at Wembley, but over the 1961-62 season was beginning to break up. Vince Karalius left, Dick Huddart went to Australia, Mick Sullivan left, Brian McGinn retired and Kenny Large finished. It was the break-up of that side and the building up of the 1964 to 1966 side. When we went to Wembley in 1966, again that side then broke up.

I've always had a good relationship with the fans. I will say this though, I don't think Saints fans are as appreciative of their own players who are born and bred in St Helens, I'm thinking of the local youngsters who come through the club. I think the fans are much harder in their criticism of them and have higher expectations than they sometimes have with an overseas player. That was a massive difference I found at Widnes, when I went there for four years, wherever you were from the fans were right behind you. Win, lose or draw there really was a very close affinity to the team. There is at Saints, but they've got some very fickle fans. There is very much a hard-core of solid support who'll be at Saints come hail, rain or snow who back the team but there is a very fickle element that comes and goes. It can sometimes undermine a side.

Before we went to Wembley in 1966, we played Hull KR at Knowsley Road in the cup and we won with a last minute, very controversial Alex Murphy try. Was it a try? I don't think it was, but I'm not grumbling about it. It was like the 1966 World Cup Final football match with West Germany, was it over the line? It would have been interesting to see what a video referee would have made of the Murphy try. It was a try that only someone like Murphy could have scored in the dying seconds. Literally a quarter of the crowd had left the ground. There had been six or seven minutes over time and in those days you didn't have a screen counting the seconds down, it was entirely up to the referee. Everybody was in suspense, nobody knew when the game would end.

We got this one last kick right by the paddock under the main stand out on the touchline. Murph put this up-and-under in and just ran like hell. Cyril Kellett was their full-back, and I think his feet were right on the dead ball line when he touched the ball. I followed Murph up, I went into the middle of the field waiting for a ricochet or something like that. I'll swear the ball was over the line when Murph jumped on it but Eric Clay, the referee was a rather portly gentleman. He was 35 yards away, the touch judge was 35 yards away and he would have had to have been a very brave man not to give that try. Clay wouldn't have bothered, he'd have disallowed it no problem. However, it would have been a very brave touch judge to disallow it. Anyway, they gave the try. It was debatable, put it that way, I'll tell you what though, I was damn glad he got it.

Hull KR were incensed over it, they really were. In fact, there was almost fighting in the bath afterwards. It really was bitter. Six weeks later, they came to play us in the Championship play-off semi-final at Knowsley Road and it was one of the most memorable matches in my time at Saints. The game was the Saturday night before we went to Wembley. Hull KR were a good, big side. They had people like Bill Holliday playing, Frank Foster in the pack and so on. They were up for it. I have never seen a side get off a coach as psyched up in my life. They were ready for revenge. Normally, even though you might knock hell out of each other on the field, you're the best of friends with the opposition off it. Before a game, you'd have a chat with them or whatever. Not this game though, they came straight down the tunnel, straight into the dressing room and locked the door. They'd come to knock us off our game thinking: "These will lie down the week before Wembley".

The first half was like the heavyweight boxing championship of the world. Everything was going on, it was mayhem. John Warlow had to go off to get stitches in a cut by his eye and just before half time we were losing. I remember the pack got together and sort of said: "What are we doing here? Are we lying down? Are we sorting this lot out? Are we going for a game or what?" We decided we were going to do them. The second half was probably the best exhibition of rugby I have ever been in. We beat them out of sight. I ended up at loose-forward, picked the ball up from the back of the scrum, went down the blind side and give it to Len Killeen who went about 60 yards to score in the corner. The ferocity in the forwards was tremendous. It was the hardest game of rugby I have ever been in throughout my life. It was physical and brutal but good rugby all the same. Beating them out of sight really set everybody up for Wembley and winning the Championship.

As a final irony in the dying seconds, Murph put up another up-and-under to Cyril Kellett. Murph was captain then. The time was up and I'd asked the ref how long was left and he'd said: "It's time Ray". I was screaming at Murph: "put the ball out or go for goal". We didn't want anybody else injured. Frankie Barrow from full-back shouted: "put an up-and-under on him", Murph was shouting: "Let's get it on him" and I'm screaming: "No, no someone could get injured". Murph puts the high ball up again and there is mayhem in the corner, I think Frankie hit him before the ball came down. The ref was trying to sort it out and I just said: "Blow time" and he said "You're right Ray" and he blew his whistle. That was the end of it but it was like World War 3. It was one hell of a game.

Winning the cup in 1966

When we won the cup in 1966, being a school teacher I had to come back early on the train with Peter Harvey on the Sunday night with the rest of the team coming back on Monday. Myself and Peter actually went to Lime Street to meet the rest of the team to bring the cup back into St Helens. You can talk about the Grand Final which has become a good occasion but the Challenge Cup has history around it, and tradition with all the years playing it at Wembley. It was something special, particularly beating Wigan at Wembley. We beat them comfortably, it was a one-horse race really. When we brought the cup back, there was also the feeling that we wanted the Championship the week after. There was a professional steel about that side. There was a good reception at the Town Hall, you get a feeling that you might be a professional player but you are also doing something for the town. You feel that you are part of the town. You really get that community feeling when the coach is coming in with the cup.

That 1966 side was certainly the most successful side I ever played in with regard to winning trophies and it certainly had a lot of talent. However, the 1961 side I signed for had equal talent to it and in some respects was even more talented individually. The first pack I ever played in was Cliff Watson, Bob Dagnall, Abe Terry, Dick Huddart, myself and Vince Karalius, and you don't get a better pack than that. Then you had Alex Murphy, Tom van Vollenhoven, Mick Sullivan and Austin Rhodes. I was very, very fortunate to play in two massively talented sides. The 1961 side was breaking up, it had enjoyed its great era from 1956 onwards. Then the 1966 side was built from 1964 onwards. It was a very professional, hard side. I mean the pack, there was something like 10 international forwards here at the time. The pack that played at Wembley had Halsall, Sayer, Watson, myself, Warlow and Mantle. You also had Kel Coslett who was injured at that time, Mervyn Hicks who played for Great Britain, you had Dougie Laughton and John Temby. There was always pressure on you. They used to rotate the forwards around, there was a lot of competition for places.

I enjoyed captaining the side after 1966, there had been a lot of controversy over Alex though, he'd gone off to Leigh as a player-coach. I'd been at Saints for six years and there was a very good spirit within the team. I had a good relationship with the coach, Joe Coan who was a very good team manager. It was a good experience to handle top international players. I think that it's a shame in today's game that the captain's role is virtually nothing. All you see today is a coach with a walkie-talkie passing on instructions to his assistants who pass it onto people masquerading as water carriers who give instructions to the players. The coach directs the players, it's like American Football. In my day, the captain gave the team talk. You were the man in charge on the field, you decided the tactics and you would even have a say with regard to substitutions. A captain had responsibility and he did have to know something about the game.

Leaving the club

The circumstances of me leaving Saints to go to Widnes were strange. I was captain and we were due to play Swinton at Swinton. The day before that game, I was painting the front of our house on a ladder. My wife got a phone call from Harry Cook and came out and told me: "Harry wants you to go to Widnes". I thought does he want me to take some tickets or brochures up there or something. I said: "Tell him I'm painting". I was up the ladder with a bucket and paint and paintbrush in my hand. My wife told him and then came back out and said: "He needs you to go to Widnes today". I said: "Won't it do next week? Tell him I'll ring him back." Anyway, I finished what I was doing and thought it's as quick just to go up there. When I went up there, Frank Myler was up there. He told me he was just sorting his terms out to sign for Saints and told me that I was going to Widnes. I said: "Am I? I didn't know that". It suddenly dawned on me what Harry Cook had been going on about. I saw Harry Cook and asked him what was going on. He said: "It's like this Ray, we've got to do this quickly, we're desperate for an inside back." Saints were, as that 1966 side was breaking up. He told me: "Widnes won't let Frank Myler go unless you go there". Widnes had a team of young kids then. I said I didn't particularly want to go but he said you'll have to. This was how Rugby League was in those days and Saints did have so many forwards. They could afford to let three go never mind one. So I went across to Widnes.

I said at the time you were like a piece of meat being sold on the market. The beauty about Saints was, at that time, that they never sold the meat when it had gone bad, they sold it when it was still sellable and attractive to others. They would sell players who had three, four or even five seasons left in them. Saints was a professional club and they always got money. They didn't let players grow old on them. Looking back, it was a tremendous move, as I captained Widnes for four years and I ended up captaining Lancashire. I went on tour with Great Britain in 1968, it was a good move for me.

34

I was offered the Saints coaching position three times. I was coaching at Cowley school for 29 years after spending three years at Fairfield in Widnes. I loved my time at Cowley, it was a great period in my life. There were some wonderful players there, people like Ian Ball, Steve Tickle, Dave Gullick, Mick Burke and so on who became professional. During my time there, I was asked to coach Salford when they had just signed David Watkins. Later, I was also asked to coach Leeds.

In fact, I can remember Tom Ellard sitting in my front room for hours on end trying to persuade me to take the Saints job. I would have loved to have done, really would have done. On the third occasion, there was no chance. On the first occasion, I had so much involvement with coaching schoolboy rugby and enjoyed it so much. I had so much going there, we were heavily involved in tours to Australia, South America and Canada. I felt I would have to give all that up. I felt as if I would be letting them down. It might have been misplaced loyalty, I don't know.

The second time was just after I had started work with the BBC and I would have had to have given that up. That wasn't really a difficult decision to make. Coaching Saints is about the only thing I've not done in rugby and I would have loved to have done it. It's the greatest regret of my life that I never coached and coached Saints in particular. If I had my time over again, I may have been a little more selfish and have done it but I can't grumble really.

The Meninga signing

Helping to sign Mal Meninga for Saints was really like an MI5, James Bond spy story. All the initial work had been done by John Clegg who was on the Saints board at that time. He'd done all the initial approaches. I thought, and this is the significant thing, that they'd hammered out a contract. I was going out on the 1984 tour to Australia covering it for BBC radio and television. I got a phone call from Saints saying: "Will you take these forms out and sign Meninga? Just keep it quiet". I thought it was quite straightforward, that was it. Was it hell! They had me under pressure for two months out there. When I got there, of course Meninga was up in Queensland, but we started the tour in Papua New Guinea. We moved onto Sydney and all round New South Wales. I was a thousand miles away from Meninga. All the time, stories were coming out that Leeds were going to sign him. Maurice Lindsay was coming over as Wigan were also after Meninga. I remember the first day in Sydney in the hotel, Joe Wareham who was general manager at Leeds and Harry Jepson had breakfast with me and they were telling me about how they were going to Brisbane to sign Mal Meninga for Leeds. Now Joe is a good friend of mine but I couldn't say a word. I had Saints' registration forms in my suitcase upstairs. All the way through the breakfast they were saying: "He'll be good for us, what do you think of him?" They were flying up to Queensland later that day. I was panicking because I couldn't follow them as I was covering the tour.

I got on the phone and I managed to track him down, he was in a training camp with Brisbane Souths who he was playing for. I said: "Look Mal, I've never met you but I've been sent over by Saints to sign you. I won't be up in Brisbane though for three weeks, I can't get there until then." He said: "Ray, don't worry, I'm signing for nobody until I've seen you, I'll promise you that." He was a man of his word all the way through, he kept his promise, an absolute gentleman and one of the nicest people I've ever met in my life. He's a good friend of mine now. All the way through the tour I heard: "Meninga's going to Leeds", or whatever. I was dreading every morning getting up, thinking if I don't sign him my name will be mud in St Helens.

When we got up there, we all stayed in this hotel in Brisbane. Maurice Lindsay had flown in by this point and Leeds had also talked with Mal. Joe Wareham said to me: "I think we've got him, we're going seeing him tomorrow". I couldn't say a word. He takes the mick out of me now saying how I led him a dance. Anyway I was thinking I've got to see this fella and fast. Leeds actually produced a press release ready for the next day saying they had signed Meninga. I rang up Wayne Bennett who was coaching Brisbane Souths then and is a real nice fella. I knew Wayne and explained the situation to him about how I needed to see Meninga. He said: "I'll tell you how we'll do it. You come midway through training and just slide into the clubhouse. Joe Wareham's coming tonight at half six supposedly to sign him and they're bringing the forms. Just wait in the clubhouse, I'll not bring them in but I'll bring Mal in after."

As I pulled up in a taxi, Joe Wareham was there and I slid round the back into the clubhouse dreading them walking through. Mal came in and I'd put on my Saints Past Players' jersey deliberately, using a bit of psychology. We sat down and we talked for about 10 minutes. I showed him the contract and we ironed a few things out. He said: "I'll sign for you." I said: "What about Leeds?" He said: "Forget it, I'll sign for you Ray." I just developed a personal rapport with him. I said: "Will you sign in here?" He said: "No, I've got to go back out training, I promise I'll sign for you," and he kept his word all the way through with everything.

He said: "I'll sign for you after the third test at Brisbane, come down into the dressing room and I'll do it there for you."

I was commentating on that match live on TV and I couldn't concentrate. I was thinking: "I've got to get his signature". I was working out how to get to the dressing rooms. Until I had that contract signed, I couldn't relax. I did the match, shot down to the dressing rooms, he hadn't come off the field. He was about to go down the tunnel and he was smiling away, he said: "Come here, give us your paper and I'll sign it". That was it. I went back to the hotel and rang Saints and said: "Get it in the press, he's signed for you". It was the most nerve-wracking period of time. If anyone ever tells you at Saints that they signed Meninga, don't believe it. John Clegg deserves a hell of a lot of credit for doing all the groundwork though.

That night Maurice Lindsay asked me if I'd signed Meninga, I told him yes and he said: "Oh bloody hell". He went off to go and get Brett Kenny to sign for Wigan. Half an hour later he came back and told me that he hadn't brought any registration forms and could I lend him one. I lent him one because Saints had given me three or four just in case I saw anyone else worth signing. I signed Phil Veivers while I was out there basically just to accompany Mal. I really liked Phil but I'll confess if I could have signed Gary Belcher

I'd have signed him before Phil Veivers. Belcher didn't want to come as he wanted to sign for Canberra Raiders. Phil turned out to be a great signing, a wonderful professional and a great servant to the club. I never looked at the form but I lent it Maurice. Three hours later, Maurice returns and he says: "Ray, you'll never bloody believe this. I've signed Brett Kenny but Saints' signatures are on the bottom. Technically, Saints have bloody signed him." He had to get this whitener to get rid of the Saints' signatures and put his one on, but Saints, technically, signed Brett Kenny. Maurice had not looked at the form and seen Saints signatures on the bottom.

Commentary

Now, with my work on radio and television, you go to Saints and you hear: "Ooh you're biased against Saints", you go to Wigan: "you're biased against Wigan", you go to Leeds: "you're biased against Leeds", wherever you go you're biased against that team. I remember a Regal Trophy match between Warrington and Oldham. I got two letters, one from a Warrington fan and one from an Oldham one. Both accused me of being biased towards the other so I photocopied the letters and sent the Warrington one to the Oldham fan and vice versa with a note saying: "make up your mind and let me know what decision you come to". I never got a reply off either of them.

Knowsley Road is a very good ground to do television from. It's a good gantry and a good viewing point. It's always good to commentate on Saints because you know you're going to get a good game of open rugby. You know that Saints will score tries and they'll let the other side score a couple.

One of the funniest things I saw at Knowsley Road was when we signed a forward called Peter Goddard from Oldham. He'd only been there about a fortnight and turned up for training with this big, brown suitcase. He was selling shirts and jerseys and so on. Mick Sullivan bought two shirts off him, two pullovers, two ties, a pair of pants, socks and the lot. It was Tuesday night training and Mick said: "I'll sort you with out with the money on Thursday when we get paid".

Well, Mick Sullivan signed for York the day after so Peter never saw him again.

Another funny incident I recall was when there was a very harsh frost in the 1962-63 season. There was no rugby played for about three months. One director, I'll not name him, was a little man and a little bit short sighted, I was stood on the sprint track where the lottery office is today. I was standing there with Bob Dagnall. Every week, this director was wondering if we were playing or if we weren't. There used to be a steel manhole cover just outside the ground. He was standing on this cover, stamping his foot saying: "They'll never play on this, it's far too hard, there's no give in it." He had no idea he wasn't on the grass. I was thinking: "He's helping pick the team, this fella'."

The game has changed totally today - although individual skill is still the same, players perform different roles and do different things now. I was a great fan of Apollo Perelini, tremendous 80-minute worker and a great team spirit player. He was a great clubman who would play when injured. Those are the type of players that I liked to play with, people like John Warlow and Cliff Watson were that type of player. Keiron Cunningham is another, you'll not see Keiron Cunningham crying off with anything. In our day you said you could go to tough places like Featherstone and Workington with players like these; I equate Perelini and Cunningham to my own era in that sense. The partnership of Long and Martyn is exciting, Anthony Sullivan's tries have been good. I like to see a wingman who can beat a man on the outside and I think Sullivan is one of the last of a dying breed in that respect. At Saints you had many great wingers who scored tries down the outside like van Vollenhoven, Llewellyn, McCormick, Killeen, Prinsloo, Carlton, Mick Sullivan and so on.

I've been involved with Saints' Past Players' Association for the past 21 years. Saints have the oldest PPA in Rugby League and we have over 270 members. It was set up by myself, Geoff Pimblett, Austin Rhodes, Stan McCormick, George Parsons and Bob Dagnall. I'm the chairman of the PPA and I think if you're building up a community club then past players should be there. Spectators like to associate with past players. It provides a social outlet for past players. St Helens, as a club, have been magnificent towards us. They are the best club in terms of looking after their past players. They pay for the lunches we have, every member gets free admission to the games. They have been 100 per cent behind it since day one. We help the club, we sponsor a player, the match ball or whatever. We help the club with its hospitality programme by having a couple of past players being interviewed at the pre-match luncheon. We give donations to schoolboy rugby, to amateur rugby, to the disabled, to anyone who suffers from an injury. We help any past player who has fallen on hard times. I think it's one of the nicest things I've been involved in.

The ground

Saints has always been one of the best grounds to play on, always been one of the best playing surfaces. It was a very wide pitch, today in Super League they're all more-or-less a standard width. In those days, you went all over the place. You could be at Batley one year on a slope at Mount Pleasant or you could be at Crown Flatt playing Dewsbury or you could be playing Whitehaven. You had to adapt to many grounds, you had to play it in the pack or your wingmen would have to come inside. Saints was always a perfect pitch, if you couldn't play rugby at Saints you couldn't play rugby at all. When it was developed from the 1940s onwards it was probably a ground that was a little bit ahead of its time. To me, it ranked alongside Headingley as the best ground. Central Park was a good ground but the pitch was poor, the River Douglas had a lot to do with that.

The whole of my life seems to be getting pulled down. I went to Knowsley Road School as a junior, that's been pulled down. The St Luke's Church Sunday School I used to go has been pulled down. I went to Cowley School as a kid and half of that has been pulled down. Now Knowsley Road is going to get pulled down. I will be disappointed because there is tradition and atmosphere. When you walk towards Knowsley Road, it's like pulling on an old overcoat or a pair of slippers, it's nice, warm, comfortable and you know everywhere. I do think it had to go as the upkeep of it was costing too much. It's a decaying fabric, it's as simple as that. The biggest problem with it is the social and hospitality facilities which is what people demand now. People want a meal and comfort and the club has got to generate income throughout the week. It will be a sad day when it does go because there are a lot of memories there.

Kel Coslett

Kel Coslett played more games for Saints than any other player, starring in 519 matches. Signed from Welsh Rugby Union in 1962, he kicked more than 1600 goals. He went on to captain the side and later became coach in 1980. He is still involved with the club in a commercial capacity.

My move to Saints came about because the club sent a scout to my mum's house in Bynea, Wales and asked if I would be interested in coming up north to play Rugby League. At that time I didn't know much about Rugby League. The next thing I knew Basil Lowe and Lionel Swift came down and signed me.

My first impression of Knowsley Road was that it was my type of stadium. It's a good ground to play on; the stands are pretty close to you. I was always used to playing on grounds like that which I preferred to Wembley or the big stadiums where the fans were far away. I enjoyed it and thought it was a good place.

My first game at Knowsley Road was against Liverpool Stanley and it was a pretty hot day. It was mid-August and the sun was belting down. It was certainly a new experience.

The crowd were very helpful, willing you to do well. They've always been on the side of new players. They were certainly very helpful and supportive to me.

The ground was good to play on and the surface was absolutely brilliant. As time went on, there was a bit of a drainage problem and it had to be returfed. The following season we had torrential rain and the turf churned up so we had one bad season on it in 1967-68. On the whole, though, it's always been very good.

Kel Coslett Testimonial Booklet (Courtesy Kel Coslett)

Before each game, I would always put my jersey on last before going
on the field and I always used to put my right boot on just before
that. When I got out I always used to kick the post for some unknown
reason. They were all little things, just habits you had.

There have been quite a few games on the ground which I have
enjoyed. One in particular was when we played Hull in the mid-
1960s. I hadn't been up here long and my mother who had never seen
me play rugby live came up for the game. We won 13-12 and it just
so happened that I kicked the winning goal. It was a big thing for me
at the time and obviously my parents enjoyed it.

Looking back at the type of players I played with, it was
frightening really. When I arrived you were next to Murphy, Huddart
and Sullivan. Then there was van Vollenhoven and Cliff Watson.
Later there was the likes of George Nicholls and Roy Mathias. It's an
endless list really.

There have been some great players I have played against as well,
the likes of Eric Ashton and Billy Boston, Bill Ramsey, Keith

42

Hepworth, Neil Fox, Syd Hynes, Dai Watkins and Jim Mills, it's endless again really. It's been a great career for me because I've been involved with so many great players.

My move from full-back to loose-forward happened by accident. I played my first two seasons at the club at full-back. I broke my leg against Rochdale at Saints on the third game of my third season in 1964-65 and it ended my season. Frankie Barrow took my place at full-back and played well. It was always difficult to get your position back because the club kept winning. We were going to Liverpool City on a Thursday night and were short of forwards. I had played stand-off at school and thought that loose-forward is not that much different. I suggested to Joe Coan who was coach at the time: "I'll have a go at loose-forward". I never looked back, I stayed there for the rest of my career and enjoyed being the link between the backs and the forwards.

I never felt too much pressure captaining the side as well as goal kicking, because you grow up into it really. I was lucky enough to captain the Welsh RU schoolboys when I was 14. It progressed from there and I was very honoured when Cliff Evans asked me to be the captain of St Helens. The initial thing was to get your first team place and after doing that to be offered the captaincy was a great honour. I enjoyed it and the goal kicking was something I'd always done so it all came together really.

It was a tremendous feeling bringing the cup back to St Helens in 1972 and 1976. You feel so proud don't you? I had been at St Helens for 10 years and had never played at Wembley. Back in the 1966 final I might not have been picked but would probably have been substitute, unfortunately I got injured the week before. You think that the chance has passed you by, because a lot of players don't get to play at Wembley. To go in 1972 after 10 years with St Helens was absolutely brilliant. To go back four years later as an ageing player was the icing on the cake.

My last game at Knowsley Road was the Premiership first round of 1976 against Wigan. Beating Wigan was always a big thing for myself and the town. We beat them then went to Wembley and beat Widnes, and then we won the Premiership final and went on tour to

Australia and New Zealand, not a bad way to finish your playing career at St Helens.

I was proud to be asked to become coach of St Helens in 1980, it was always my ambition to come back to Knowsley Road and coach. Obviously, there was a lot of work to be done. Possibly, what happened at Saints was similar to what happened at Wigan in that the good players were allowed to get old together without the young players being brought in. Whether that was a cashflow problem I don't know.

The current side has some good players. There's the two centres Iro and Newlove. They've got Long, Martyn and Chris Joynt, all good players. Good players are able to adapt. For example, if they change a rule, you adapt to it.

I still see some of the side I played with thanks to the Past Players' Association. We meet up four times a year. It's nice to have a chat with players you've played with and against.

My current role is on the commercial side as all sports need sponsorship. I'm here to get as much sponsorship as possible. When they do get here we have to make sure they enjoy the game, the atmosphere and the hospitality. You want them walking away saying: "I enjoyed that and I'll come back".

If someone had a magic wand, you could knock the stadium down and rebuild it on the same spot because it's an ideal place. You've got to move forward with the times though. You've got to look to the future and play in a new stadium.

John Mantle

John Mantle signed for Saints in December 1964 and played in more than 450 games. A big, fast forward, he joined the club from Newport Rugby Union. He played in many finals and was an integral part of the 'Dad's Army' side that beat Widnes at Wembley in 1976.

Saints had been down watching me at Newport and in those days of course you daren't even whisper about being approached by a Rugby

League club. Then the chairman Harry Cook and vice-chairman Charlie Martin came down to the house and we discussed terms. I'd always fancied the game. It was an opportunity to repay my parents who had struggled to put me through college. I think I made the right decision, whether I made it a little prematurely I don't know. It's pure conjecture really but it's been said and written about that I would have made the British Lions RU touring side the following year. As it happened, I toured with the Rugby League Lions just over a year after I had signed. Looking back now, I would have liked to have toured with the RU Lions but you make your decisions and stand by them. Just prior to signing for Saints I had been picked for the Barbarians for their Christmas tour. I was never a big fan of the Barbarians as they were very snobbish. I remember David Watkins, they thought he had claimed too much in expenses from them and never picked him again.

First impressions

I was reasonably impressed with Knowsley Road as a ground, I had seen it on television. I was at college with a St Helens lad who I shared with when I first came up. The playing surface was pretty good, the stands were like most of the grounds at that time. It compared with Newport quite favourably really.

What I remember about my first game for Saints was scoring two 75-yarders against Wigan's A team. All I can remember was that there was quite a sizeable crowd on. It was also Kel Coslett's first game back after a broken leg. The crowd for that A team game, believe it or not, was more than 9,000. My signing had garnered quite a lot of publicity, it had made television and so on. It had been reported as another one leaves the valleys.

I had been selected as vice-captain of the Welsh Union side. I didn't know that until after I had signed, whether that would have changed my mind I don't know. Before that Wigan A team game I had not even trained with the team. My first introduction to the play-the-ball rule was in a corridor with the A team coach Steve Llewellyn. It was: "When you get tackled keep hold of the ball and play it with your foot through your legs." I was very fit, reasonably fast for a big fella, I could do 100 yards in about 10 seconds. I was Welsh triple jump champion at under-15s, 17s and 19s age level. I was ranked in the top four in Great Britain. Then I went to college and put too much weight on to continue doing it.

The only other thing I remember about the Wigan game was that they had a fella playing for them called Peter Davies. Wigan had signed him instead of me. Wigan had come down to watch me play for Newport against Neath. In those days, Neath were a bunch of animals in my opinion. They would bite, kick, punch, you name it. On that particular night, the Neath pack were trying every dirty trick and I was the only Newport forward who stood up to them. I was very sore after that match I can tell you. Wigan signed Peter Davies. So, in that first A team match I scored two 75-yarders as I say and he was diabolical. He never lasted the season so Saints came out of the deal far better, so they say.

The crowd treated me very well. Obviously I couldn't have had a better start than scoring two 75-yarders against Wigan. I think the crowd appreciated my work rate. I mean I was a runner but I got through a lot of tackling as well. The stats today make me laugh. I remember a game I watched when Ellery Hanley was playing for Wigan and they were saying: "He has actually made 44 tackles this game". I used to average more than that every game. I think the top one that was recorded for me was 56 tackles. Kel Coslett and I were always the top two and more often that not, it was me that was top. Most of my tackles were first tackles whereas a few of the team were very good at coming in second man and making a tackle that way.

I was the first player there on match day 95 per cent of the time. Being a PE specialist, I was obviously very aware of the importance of warm up. I had quite an arduous warm-up really. Tony Karalius would turn up 10 minutes before kick-off, have a cigarette and go out and play. He used to watch me warm-up and say: "You're going to be shattered". I never did a hamstring or pulled a muscle throughout my career. Obviously it works and preparing in the right way was a big thing for me. I was never outwardly nervous, but I felt the nerves just like everyone else. Obviously we weren't as conscious of diet in those days but I was never one for eating heavily before a match. I would just have some toast and jam to get a bit of energy into me.

Big games and coaching

The Wigan games were always the ones you looked forward to. They were the ones you enjoyed, even though they were invariably harder than the average game. Obviously it's the local derby isn't it? Another game that stands out is in 1966 when we won everything and we played Hull KR at home in the cup and we won in the last minute. The club games against the Australians all stand out, I never lost against the Aussies for Saints.

I had the middle finger on my left hand amputated in the June of one year and we played the Aussies in the September. I had a big abscess on my hand and the doctor said: "You can't play". I replied: "You try and stop me". I always loved playing against the Aussies. I remember during that game hitting Bobby Fulton and the pain in my hand was tremendous. The next day I had to have the abscess drained by having a big needle shoved down it. We had a weakened side that day and still beat the Aussies. I got man-of-the-match that day and I never had a bad game against the Aussies.

In the early days I received no coaching as such from any Saints coach. The first bit of coaching I received was from one of the opposition coaches, Roy Francis from Leeds. He was way ahead of his time. It was something like late February, early March and we played Leeds at Saints. I had a good game, I made a few breaks and ran onto the ball. After the game, Roy said to me: "You're making breaks in the hard part of the field, why not try running a bit wider out?" Then people used to say to me: "Why are you running at centres?" The simple answer was that it was the smartest thing to do. I am amazed at some of today's forwards who run at the nearest tackler rather than at the gap. If you run at the gap, it's less painful and if you draw two men in and get rid of the ball it creates chances. I mean, Tommy Bishop used to be glued to me to receive the ball after I made a break.

The only other coaching I received that I would call coaching - speaking as someone who has coached at a professional level - was from Cliff Evans. He came from Swinton at a time when Swinton were a good club who played good rugby. He brought a lot to Saints, a lot of moves and so on.

Joe Coan, although he will go down as one of the most successful Saints coaches ever, would probably be the first to admit he wasn't a coach in the true sense of the word. He was all about fitness. If he made Saints fitter than any other team it would work for him. He used to really flog us in training. It got the right results. Training was boring though, it wasn't very well thought out. His instructions were to hammer them in the forwards for 60 minutes with our good, big pack. Then in the last 20, we let the backs score the tries. It worked.

In 12 seasons I played in 19 finals including 10 Championship finals, the end of season play-offs. Not many players have done that. It makes me laugh when I hear people talking about the number of games players have to play today, they're full-time professionals. We would play far more games and weren't as advantaged as the modern player. I would like to have seen the players of my era have had the opportunities that the modern players have, then you'd have some super players. Cliff Watson was faster than most of the second rows that you have today, then there was Albert Halsall. He was quick over 30 yards. Then of course Dougie Laughton and myself. At our best, we were faster than the backs. I used to beat the Great Britain wingers in training on tour on the Sydney Cricket Ground. Of course the game is faster today. The thing that disappoints me is the amount of tries that are let in. We used to pride ourselves on our defence, we used to let in an average of seven or eight points a game over a whole season.

Standout players

Players who stand out are obviously van Vollenhoven and to a lesser extent Len Killeen. Voll was the ultimate wingman. I have seen a lot of wingers in both codes and he was probably the most complete all-round winger of them all. As an attacker he was outstanding, he could do 100 yards in 9.6 seconds, he was so quick. He was also strong defensively, he was unbelievable.

Bob Prosser, who was my team-mate at Newport as well as at Saints, was a brilliant footballer. He was one of the longest passers of the ball you'll ever see. He would miss three or four men out to send a 30 or 40 yard ball out to me, I would just run onto it hitting the centres at pace. Before I signed for Saints, I was on the verge of breaking the Newport try scoring record and a lot of that was down to Bob's passing. Frank Myler was another player who was under rated, he would very often put me through gaps with his passing, I wouldn't have to find them, he would just send me through. Billy Benyon was a good player although he lacked pace, a tremendous defensive centre and also a good wingman's centre. Then there was John Walsh. There is probably no-one who is as slow as John was who had the same success. He may not have had pace but he had a rugby brain. He was a hard man and a real character - what a player, thinking wise, he was three weeks ahead of everybody else on a rugby field.

Dougie Laughton and Cliff Watson were both tremendous. Obviously there was Kel Coslett, a good player and organiser. I was lucky I suppose to play with so many class players. That was one of the criteria though for me when I came to Rugby League, I wanted to join a strong side. The game was hard enough without coming to a struggling side.

As for the opposition, obviously there were lots of good forwards playing in those days. I always liked playing against Colin Dixon at Salford who later became my team mate when I went to the Willows later in my career. There was also Peter Smethurst who played for Oldham and Wigan among other clubs. He was my type of forward, you could hit lumps out of one another, nothing dirty, just part of the game. We would give each other hell and just smile at each other. There would be a few funny comments exchanged.

Brian Edgar helped me and was an influence on me. He was a big Cumbrian lad who played for Workington. He was a tremendous forward, he was a ball player and could also run a bit. He also hated the Aussies off the field and on it.

There were a lot of forwards in those days who would use the elbow. I had 40 or 50 stitches as a result of being elbowed in the face during my career at Saints.

John Mantle Testimonial Brochure
(Courtesy John Mantle)

My career at Knowsley Road ended in good style in 1976. We went to Wembley and beat Widnes, beat Salford in the Premiership final and then toured Australia and New Zealand. We didn't go straight away, if we had done that we would have had more success. We waited six weeks before going over there and looking back that cost us. A few of the lads had been celebrating after our successes back home, although we did do reasonably well when we got over there.

The Wembley game was a lasting memory. The week before I had been over to Widnes for a sporting forum and was getting all sorts of questions like: "How will you keep up with the young Widnes pack?" The press continued along the same theme and yet I was only 34 and was very fit. We ran the legs off them on a very hot day. It was more than 100 degrees Farenheit and I loved it. I really enjoyed it and didn't want to come off but Eric Ashton wanted to give Mel

James a run because he had never played at Wembley. I was never tired that day even though I lost half a stone due to the heat.

Out of the current lads, I rate Tommy Martyn as probably the most complete all-round footballer in Super League. He would have been a good player in our time. Sean Long settled in very quickly and has got better as time has gone on. I like Chris Joynt, his work rate is good and he has some pace. Over 30 yards he's probably quicker than I was but over a distance I'd overtake him I would have thought. I like to see Sully beating people for pace on the outside and some days he's excellent. His finishing is second to none. Newlove, when he plays, is good to watch.

I don't go to that many games nowadays and instead watch matches on the box. I have had one knee re-built and the other is nearly ready to be done, if I stand for so long I can't move and the seats in the stand are in too confined a space. I still follow the side and want them to do well though. I also keep in touch with the Past Players' Association.

What has amazed me after being involved with Saints for 30 years is the amount of young players who sign for the club and never make it. It is phenomenal and you think questions would be asked. I'm talking about players signed at a junior level, who progress to the academy, go through the A team and get a regular first team place. You'd be lucky if it was 10 per cent who made it out of the lads they signed in the 1970s and 1980s. In business, questions would certainly be asked. I did a centre of excellence for BARLA and we used to get the cream of amateur Rugby League. There used to be some very good young players and I would try to put a few of them Saints way but Saints wouldn't be willing to pay the extra money and they ended up at Warrington or Wigan.

The club is not going out of existence, you have to move with the times. They're just moving headquarters. Knowsley Road is an antiquated stadium. When I first arrived, I remember how small the changing rooms were and the bath was poor, the facilities weren't great.

Billy Benyon

Billy Benyon was a centre for Saints in the 1960s and 1970s and played 510 times for the club, appearing in more than 20 finals. He left to join Warrington as a player, but returned to Saints in 1982 as coach bringing the Lancashire Cup and Premiership Trophy to the club in the 1984-85 season. Despite this success, he was sacked from the coaching position in November 1985.

1961 was my first game, we played Rochdale Hornets at home. I remember they had quite a few large Fijians in the side and I think I played stand-off. I was about 17 and it was fantastic at the time. You'd achieved an ambition and running out at Knowsley Road as part of the Saints side was great.

Of course I was a local lad and I think the St Helens crowd has an affinity with any local lad who makes it there. If they see talent in one then they respond to it. I think all through my time there I had a good rapport with them.

St Helens' playing surface has always been renowned as one of the best in the game. Even playing there as a schoolboy you realise it although it's only afterwards that you realise how good the surface really was. The club in a lot of ways must take some credit for the people they've appointed to look after the pitch over the years.

In one sense, I feel lucky that I played with some tremendous players both in the 1960s and the 1970s. In the 1960s side I was one of the youngest players - you're looking up to players that you're actually playing with. I wouldn't say as a kid that I was a keen Saints supporter as I used to play football in school. Once you heard the names of van Vollenhoven and Alex Murphy though it was great to be part of that set-up. It was always an achievement just to be in a Saints side.

In my early days one certain player said to me that I wasn't there to score tries I was there to give the ball to Tommy Voll or Len Killeen who were the wingers. It was my responsibility to give them the ball as quickly and as cleanly as possible. It was something of a bonus if I scored. In the early days I was quiet in the dressing room, I just used to listen to what other people required of you. As time went on I started to do a lot of talking and encouraging players even though at times I wasn't captain of the side. As time goes on you change. You always would have your quiet moments of course but things did change and I felt the better for it. It was good when you could openly say things and talk to the younger players who were coming through as well.

Saints played in a final of some type every year which was a major achievement. We had the confidence to help us along. To go to Wembley and beat the biggest rivals Wigan in 1966 was brilliant. We had a certain cockiness and arrogance through the side at the time. Even now, it brings the hairs up on the back of your neck thinking about that occasion. Deep down in your memory, it's one that you'll treasure for a long, long time.

The 1976 final holds a pride of place in my heart as well. The nucleus of that side was local talent. In fact throughout the era of Saints' great success all strong St Helens sides had a backbone of home-grown talent.

As for the games that stand out at the ground? Going back and beating them! No, just joking. There are so many games I played in at the ground not just with Saints but with Lancashire and Great Britain. I used to enjoy Saints' matches with the tourists as we were very successful against any touring sides. You always felt that each game was of real importance though. I enjoyed playing in every game to be honest.

One of the players I hold a tremendous amount of respect for is Tom van Vollenhoven, both on and off the field. He was a gentleman, he gave you time, he would listen to you, encourage you and help you. I don't think anyone comes up to the measure of him.

The circumstances of why I did leave reflect one of the sad points that St Helens seems to have. I'd had a back injury and had been in hospital. I was given clearance to play and was told that the club had accepted terms from Warrington for me. This was the first I'd heard of it. In their mind, they'd had the best out of me and I was going. It's one of the issues I've seen since going out of the game, loyalty is never repaid. That was one of the main things that a coach would instil into a player that you had to have loyalty to the club. You just don't see it today and it's sad.

Coming back as coach

As a player I went away from the club on unhappy terms, but it was fantastic to come back as coach. Meninga was a great player but I like to emphasise that he was one great player amongst other great players in that side of 1984-85. It's sad that people don't give the recognition to the local players who were in that team. The nucleus of that side were eight or nine St Helens-born players. There was the likes of Harry Pinner, Neil Holding, Steve Peters, Roy Haggerty and Andy Platt. It was a side that came together and that was in my third year as coach. I felt a lot of the foundation work had been laid. I'd persevered and worked with the talent that was at the club.

I felt I was getting the side right which it was, without a shadow of a doubt. We beat sides with quality football. I was lucky enough to have good players to coach and train. Different opinions were held within the club after Meninga, then there was confrontation and after that it was only a matter of time before I left.

Eric Chisnall

Eric Chisnall is a St Helens man who played 495 times for his home-town team. He played second-row for the side, making his debut in 1967, and was part of the side that brought back the Challenge Cup to St Helens in 1976.

I had trials at Wigan when I first started playing. Their scout invited me down. But Len Kilshaw from Saints used to go round doing insurance work, you know door-to-door. He went to Mitchell's Ice Cream place and I used to mate about with the Mitchell lad. The Mitchells told Kilshaw: "It looks well when a St Helens lad has to go Wigan for a game." So Len Kilshaw asked him: "Who are you on about?" and he said: "Eric Chisnall". The second game I had at Wigan, Saints sent a scout down to watch me. On the Sunday after, there was a knock on the door and it was Basil Lowe inviting me down to speak to Mr Cook. They said: "Whatever Wigan offer you we'll give you more". I had my third trial and told Wigan I didn't want to sign for them and I signed for Saints. It wouldn't have gone down well in our house if I had signed for Wigan, the old lady would have disowned me.

At the time of making my debut for Saints in 1967 I was working at Pilks contracting. I was at work and someone came up to me and told me I was playing in a midweek game for the club. I don't remember much about my actual debut for the club, your first game just goes over your head to be honest. I was lucky, I was a Saints speccie one minute then playing in the first team the next. They still had the likes of van Vollenhoven and Tommy Bishop.

The crowd was always good with me, there was never any problem with the speccies. Saints has a good pitch and a good atmosphere with it being close to the speccies. The only other pitch you can compare to Saints with regard to playing on is Leeds.

I never really had any pre-match routines that I followed, I was never superstitious in any way until I broke my arm in 1976. Someone said to me: "It's unlucky to go out behind someone who's got red hair." I don't know why they said it but of course we had Roy Mathias and Les Jones playing for us at the time and going out onto the pitch I would make sure I was never behind them.

One game that stands out for me at Knowsley Road is my first county game. I played for Lancashire against Cumberland. That was one that stood out. I had not long signed for Saints before playing in that. Obviously there are a load of cup ties that stand out as well.

It's a dream come true for any local lad to bring the Challenge Cup back from Wembley isn't it? It's something that everyone wants to do and something I'll never forget, it's just unbelievable. [Eric Chisnall was a member of the 1972 and 1976 Saints cup-winning teams].

Speaking as a forward, I have to mention Cliff Watson and John Mantle. John Mantle was something a bit special. A lot of local lads played at that time, such as Billy Benyon who was a good player.

There were some cracking opposition players as well at that time. One of the best was Alex Murphy, he went to Leigh after leaving Saints then he went to Warrington. Steve Nash who played for Featherstone and Salford was a good player. There were also good forwards like Ray Batten and Bob Haigh of Leeds.

My last game at Knowsley Road wasn't such a great game. It was a cup match against Wigan, we got beaten and I shouldn't have been playing, I was injured. Kel Coslett asked me if I could play so I did. Wigan weren't very good then so losing to them was a sickener.

Out of the current side I rate Cunningham as by far the best player in the country. He does things when there's nothing on. Sean Long is another one who can do something when nothing's happening. They can turn a game on their own.

As for the strangest thing I've seen at Knowsley Road I have to say those dogs they have walking round now. Who'd have thought we'd ever have dogs on the pitch?

I think they should have redeveloped the current site instead of moving. You could have developed the Edington end and the clubhouse end to become all-seater. Then you still have your people who stand up on the popular side of the ground. In an all-seater stadium, you lose the tradition of being able to stroll on and find your mates and watch the game with them in the same place. In an all-seater stadium, you sit where you're told. You've got to have comfort but if people want to stand up they should have that choice. You only have to look at the popular side at Knowsley Road now, they're all stood together and when they get going they get the team going. The players hear the speccies and they respond to it. I think the move's a bit sad, you've got a cracking pitch, adequate parking. I accept the stadium needs upgrading but surely they could have found the money. But St Helens Rugby League Club is still the best club in the world in my opinion.

Geoff Pimblett

Geoff Pimblett was Saints' full-back in the team of the 1970s that set Rugby League alight and enjoyed unparalleled success for the club.

He signed from St Helens Rugby Union in 1971 and played his last game for the club on 1 April 1979, having amassed more than 300 appearances and more than 600 goals for the club. His career included two Wembley successes in 1972 and 1976. He is currently the secretary of the Saints Past Players' Association.

When I signed for Saints, in those days, you didn't go automatically into the first team because they had such a good side. I played about eight or nine A team games which were a little bit better supported than they are today but you didn't really make an impact at all. When I got my chance in the late February of that season the crowd were very, very good to me. I think they wanted to see some new people in the side, some players were just reaching the end of their careers. They had Frankie Barrow at full-back and he'd had 10 good years.

That was the four tackle rule era and that lent itself to a running full-back style of play rather than a defensive one. The team was doing well that year and in fact from late February onwards I ended up playing until the last game of the season which was Wigan in the Championship Final and we never lost. So, we were on top, things were going well and the crowd was fully behind us. Obviously you have various blips over the years because not all speccies like your style of play. Luckily in the 1970s we were a very successful side, you rolled your little spells of poor form and the odd comment from the popular side or behind the sticks. The crowd were great with me, I'm a St Helens lad and I think they appreciated that as well. You're Saints red and white eyeballs yourself sort of thing.

Debut game

My first home game at Knowsley Road I played stand-off and we won. However, a few games along when we played Wigan at Central Park on Good Friday I was picked at full-back and stayed there for 99 per cent of my time at Saints.

I remember my debut for Saints, it was Whitehaven away. The pitch was like red mud and you changed in a little railway pavilion and you walked from there through the crowd onto the pitch. At half-time you didn't go back there, you went under the wooden stand to get taped up or get a cup of tea. I was sub that day and the first half I had been sitting on the bench. Second half, I made my debut and I thought what the hell am I coming to here? It's supposed to be professional and I'm under a wooden stand with a mud floor holding a cup of tea waiting to get belted in the second half. I came on as centre because that was my position for Lancashire Rugby Union.

I don't know whether the directors had had a word but in that second half, the stand-off Frank Myler kept shovelling the ball to me. The whole second half, I was either tackling them or getting hammered but I had to do it. I was glad in a way, I think I made 15 tackles in the second half which is a lot really. Whether it was coincidence that the ball was coming that way or whether Frank Myler was shovelling it along, I don't know. I remember it distinctly. I remember after the game we'd won and we walked back through the crowd. Anyone in the crowd can have a go at you, can't they? They did with John Wall years later, someone hit him with an umbrella.

My first home game was against Swinton. I remember John Mantle, who was a marvellous player, said to me: "follow me". Sure enough he made a bit of a break and he was quick John, I backed up, inside to Alan Whittle who was scrum-half and he was in under the sticks in the first five minutes. You're in the game then and people in the crowd are talking: "There's that new lad, he's done something already". So, I've a lot to thank John for. Obviously I was still learning the game but you'd proved that you had got something.

Grounds

Knowsley Road was always one of the best three grounds in Rugby League. Wigan had its ups and downs, it could either be a great surface or a blooming mud-heap at times. They wrecked their pitch when they installed the under-soil heating. Us and Leeds I rated as having the best playing surfaces. It's not just the surface though, it's the atmosphere. I always liked Bradford, you're down in the dip, it's a big pitch, plenty of running about. It was always a bit soft but it

58

was good to play on. Yet at Widnes, it was always a tip, you could never get comfortable in it somehow. There was Station Road, Swinton with its massive pitch, of course it's gone now. They always used to play the big games there so that's another good pitch to play on for different reasons.

At Knowsley Road, we'd like playing towards the tunnel, as it was then, in the second half, the boy's pen. There was no real advantage in which end you played to as it was such a level, flat pitch.

I remember in 1971 I played in 55 games and there was about half a dozen others who were up there with me in playing 50 games or more. You have to remember, we were part-time professionals. Having said that, the game has changed and it's unfair to compare with today's game and the amount of matches they play. In those days, if you played, you got paid and if you didn't play you got something but it wasn't really worth having. So that was an encouragement to want to play.

We were also a successful side, in addition to all the league games, you had the Floodlit Trophy with four or five games on the way, Wembley with four or five games to get there, then there's the Premiership. So you're building up your games all the time. I think if you stay clear of injury, you're not thinking: "Oh I've played 40 games now" or whatever. It doesn't work that way. I think if you're injured or carrying a knock it might start to become a factor. I don't think you could play as many games today because the game has changed. The style has changed, there's not as many slow passages of the game these days.

Before the game, lads had different ways of doing things. Some kept out of the changing rooms until the last 20 minutes when the coach was there. It only took them about 10 minutes to get changed. I used to get there about 40 minutes before. I took my time and I always used to wear my old college shirt underneath.

I didn't wear shoulder pads but I had a proper jersey underneath my Saints shirt. I had that old college jersey for years and years. I always wore it when playing, it ended up as a rag but it didn't matter, I always used to wear it. You liked to do things in the same way without a doubt. I always put my boots on before I put my shorts on. I could just slip my shorts on right at the end.

Wembley magic

Bringing the cup back to Knowsley Road in 1972 and 1976, well they were magic days. 1972 was quite strange in a way, I'd only been at the club five minutes, I was only someone there to make up the numbers. I didn't have an important part to play in many ways. 1972 was significant though because it was the last year that the team coach actually went down Empire Way, they re-routed it after that year. The bus is crawling down and all your speccies are there. You know everyone: "there's so and so" and whatever. You think to yourself: "They've paid a lot of money these lads to come here". What if we get pasted? How disappointed will they all be as well, of course, as yourself. After that, you didn't see the spectators again that close. I remember that though more than anything about Wembley that year. Of course we had Graham Rees, God rest his soul, going in for the quickest try at Wembley, after charging down Hepworth's kick.

Coming back with the cup was just fantastic. You had bloody big photographs on the bus. You used to stop in a pull-in on the M6 and change from the coach to the open top bus. You started off at Haydock and went all the way round the town. In 1972 and 1976, for the next month or so, you took the cup round to all the pubs. So, if someone said: "Can we have the cup tonight?" you'd just go along with it. It was a different thing altogether. I was a teacher and I took it to school with me, all the kids had their photograph taken with it. It was a big part of the town. At these times, all the town was decorated with red and white. In recent years, the town hasn't had that red and white look on it on Wembley day. Of course, when you come back, you're on the town hall steps, spouting forth and it's a good occasion. For one of the finals, we actually got sent off to Wembley from Knowsley Road. We used to have a proper send-off, marvellous occasions.

Players

The best side I played in at Saints was over two season, 1974-75 and 1975-76. It ended up with the 1976 Wembley victory and the Championship and all that business. After that it broke up as a few of the older ones left. That rivals the 1961 side, the 1966 side that won four cups and, of course, the 1996 side that did the double. That 1976 side though was up there with them. We had Kel Coslett who, of course, was the organiser, points scorer, everything came off him. John Mantle, without doubt, was the finest forward that I ever played with. John was 16 stone 5 pounds and fit as a butcher's dog. He could run, tackle and, if someone needed sorting, John could do it. Eric Chisnall was a marvellous footballer, quick and full of ability. George Nicholls, who we bought the season after Wembley in 1972, was a wonderful player, all action. He played for Great Britain 20 odd times. As for the backs, good heavens above. We had John Walsh and Billy Benyon in the centre, later on Eddie Cunningham had a marvellous two years here in the centre. He was wonderful, he scored 30 odd tries one year. He was very much a bustling, aggressive, darting quick centre. I've not mentioned Les Jones and Roy Mathias who scored more than 200 tries between them.

There were also plenty of great players for the opposition over the years. In my day, not so much now, clubs had wingers, pairs of wingers who would be with the club for season after season. As a full-back I was always aware of the wingers I would be facing. There was Smith and Atkinson of Leeds, they played for 10 years together. For Salford, you had Maurice Richards and Keith Fielding. I mean, Fielding was an international sprinter, you couldn't give him any room. They were great players in their own way. And you had Roger Millward at Hull KR, he was a good 'un.

As for the forwards, there's a load really but two or three come to mind. Malcolm Reilly of Castleford, bloody good footballer, could put in little chip kicks. You name it, he could do it. Bill Ashurst of Wigan once produced the best second-row display I've ever seen in the 1971 Championship Final against us when we beat them in the last 10 minutes with a controversial try from Billy Benyon. That day,

Ashurst ran me all over the place and I never touched the ball. It was the four tackle rule and he kicked it from one side of the pitch to the other. I was jiggered and I'd not done anything. Then he went to Australia and played a number of seasons there. He came back with two dodgy knees, played for Wakefield and he still played well. If you put your mind to it, you could think of a lot more. There was Syd Hynes as well at Leeds, always a nasty piece of work but another good player. There was Phil Lowe at Hull KR, another tough one to play against. He was a runner and you were always going to meet him at some point in the game.

Big games

Out of the home fixtures I played, the international matches always stand out. We beat the Australians, you know, in our day. In the later years, whether it was injuries or whether it was political, we had weakened sides against them. You weren't thrashed but you got beaten. I enjoyed playing against the Australians and New Zealanders. In our day, our Saints side beat both of those sides. Beating a test team at home was always a good occasion. Then there was the Wigan game of course, it didn't matter where they were played. They were funny games as well. Wigan in those days were a good side, but not the top team, yet they could come to Saints and beat us when we were riding high. I remember one year when we got beaten by them. They kicked off, I picked the ball up. I got tackled by Green Vigo, it was a normal tackle but the ball popped up. They picked it up and scored. We'd only been going two seconds and we were down. It was one of those games when you try your darndest and nothing goes right for you. I was hitting goals and I got a few of them but there were some I was hitting just right but they were only just missing. We only got beaten by a point as well.

I remember Bill Francis doing me up here one year. I think we drew that day. Later on, Bill signed for us and had a marvellous couple of years. He was a stand-off and he had me right on the 25-yard line in the middle of the field. I thought he could only step off his right foot. So I went that way, of course, he stepped off his left and went straight under the posts. I felt a blooming idiot, there were 12 or 13,000 at the ground. I always enjoyed the Salford games as well. They had such a marvellous back line with Paul Charlton at full-back, David Watkins, Steve Nash at scrum-half. Mike Coulman in the pack but no-one else really as strong as he was even though they were a decent pack. The Warrington games were always a scrap. It was always a hard game but they're local derbies, fair enough. Widnes of course, started to become a good side in the seventies and that lasted until the early nineties when they had to sell off their players.

If a game was on the television, it affected your build-up in a way. In those days, the games would be on a Saturday afternoon and they would televise the second half. So, you'd be waiting in the tunnel and you'd have the TV fella counting you down. You had to be patient, you were all built up then you had to calm down because this bloke's saying: "Wait two minutes because there's a race late from so and so". The big games when you went out through the tunnel, you'd done all your talking. You'd feel right in your head and you just want to get out there and do it. Once you're on that field and the noise hits you, you're all right then.

To be honest, I can't remember my last game at Knowsley Road as when I played it I had no idea it was going to be my last match there. It was 1979 and I think we still finished fourth or fifth but we'd had a few bad results. We were due to play Wakefield in the semi-final of the Cup and we had three away games on the trot. We lost them all, we were going through a bad spell. At the time, Eric Ashton was coach and of course I was captain of the club. At Tuesday night's training he sort of said: "Geoff I think you should have a rest, you're not playing so well" type of thing. He left me out of the semi-final side. I finished my career then, I was going to finish anyway, I think there was about seven games left until the end of the season but the decision had been made for me. My last game for the club was 1 April 1979 at Wakefield.

The strangest thing that ever happened to me at Knowsley Road is that I had a spell of getting a bang during the games. I would carry on playing but only sort of come to at half time with no recollection of

63

the first half. It wouldn't happen these days because they'd take you off. I remember a game against Warrington on a Friday night, it was a half seven kick-off. I looked at the clock and it was twenty-five to eight, we'd just kicked off. I looked at the clock again and it was five minutes past eight and I thought there's something not quite right here. I'd missed the first half, it happened for three consecutive games.

The strangest thing that happened to me away from Knowsley Road was my last match against Wakefield. In those days, the crowd were very close to the pitch. We had scored and I was lining up the conversion from right out wide on the touchline. As I'm preparing to kick it, a little lad jumps out of the crowd and boots the ball. That's it, concentration gone.

Which of today's side would have got in the 1970s team? Well, they've got a few good lads there now haven't they? You must take into account that it's a different sort of game but also considering that good players will be able to play in any situation. Both centres, Iro and Newlove are world class. Don't get me wrong, we had two good centres. Newlove and Iro were no better than the two centres that we had but they could have come in and played. Joynty would have got a game in our team and I rated Apollo when he was at the club. Keiron Cunningham is a good player, he's world class in fact. Now we had Tony Karalius who was a different style of hooker. He wasn't a bustling, powerful type of player like Keiron. Keiron would have got into our team. I've missed some good players out like Anthony Sullivan but we had two good wingers.

I am involved with the club's Past Players' Association as secretary. We have about 250 members and a strong committee with Ray French as chairman with Austin Rhodes and Peter Harvey. We're not an old fogies type of gang, we want the younger players to join when they finish their time at the club. I suppose the difference these days is that players don't stay as long at any one club. At Saints, there's probably Joynty and Anthony Sullivan along with Keiron of course who have been here a while. These days you're three years here, three years somewhere else. We have got some recent stars in our ranks, Bobbie Goulding signed up and Danny Arnold joined.

When the rumours of a move away from Knowsley Road started, I thought, they can't do this, they can't pull Knowsley Road down after all the years of history. There's so many memories, great players, big occasions and so on. Thinking about it as time went on though, we are in the 21st century and we want a stadium for the next 100 years. The Rugby League side will always be the dominant partner in the set-up of a stadium for the town. The town is only known for two things, glass and Saints. Knowsley Road is a lovely ground though and a good seeing ground for the speccies. It's a great ground for playing on also.

George Nicholls

George made 265 appearances for Saints after joining from his home-town team Widnes in January 1973. George was a popular second-rower who was part of the Great Britain World Cup-winning side of 1972. He remains the only man to win the Man of Steel, the Lance Todd Trophy and the Harry Sunderland Trophy.

When I signed from Widnes the Saints crowd received me very well. I live in Widnes, it's my home town and I never wanted to leave. In those days you all liked to play for your home town. I think at the time Widnes needed the money though and I was playing international Rugby League. Saints were obviously interested and came in for me. It was one of those things, it was only with knowing a few people at Saints, that helped because I would never have travelled. I was happy to go to Saints in the end and had a good nine seasons there.

Knowsley Road has always been a place that I enjoyed playing at. As a player, you knew it was one of the top grounds.

One of the happiest moments of my Saints career was when we went to Wembley in 1976 and beat Widnes. I had a point to prove. I still lived in Widnes and all my friends and family supported Widnes. That was a great occasion that day.

The 1976 team I played in was the best team I ever played with. We played for one another, if someone made a mistake someone else would be there to cover for them.

I was always nervous before games, no matter how many games I played, whether it be a league or cup game, I was nervous. I always felt it was a good point for me feeling nervous. There would be the odd occasion where you didn't feel nervous and they were the times when you got too confident. So I was glad to feel nervous but as soon as I went down the tunnel onto the pitch, all the nerves would be gone. Saints have always been a good team and I have a lot of happy memories there.

Harry Pinner

Harry Pinner made 332 appearances for Saints over an 11-year period, making his debut in 1976. He was captain of the side for most of the 1980s and had a big influence on the side with his play-making abilities. Known as a skilful ball-playing forward he was a favourite of the Saints supporters. He also captained Great Britain.

My first game at Knowsley Road was in March 1976 against Wakefield, who had a big pack at the time. The difference between A team football and first team football was definitely the pace of the game. Playing for your home club, being a local lad, was fantastic.

I always got on well with the St Helens crowd, I had my critics as every player does. I thought I was well-liked although I don't mean that in a big-headed sort of way. The crowd like local lads coming through and doing quite well.

Knowsley Road was my favourite ground because it was my home ground and you always seem to play better at home for some reason. When the crowd got behind you, it made a hell of a difference.

When I first came into the side I played with a lot of talented players such as George Nicholls, he was very good with me. He led by example as skipper. Then there was Billy Benyon who was a good captain and player. I just tried to captain the way they had. I relished the responsibility of being captain. Mind you, I wasn't mad on doing the goal-kicking but we were short of a kicker so I did it. I really enjoyed being captain though.

I did have a few offers from other clubs during my time at Saints, obviously Wigan was one. I thought Saints wanted to sell me to Wigan at one point in my career, it was a misunderstanding that ended with me staying away from the club. That was probably wrong but I was that type of person. It got blown up out of all proportion. They put me on the list for a world record fee. Steve Norton had gone to Hull for £25,000 and I went on at £95,000. Saints were just trying to frighten off interested clubs. I didn't want to go as I was a Saints lad through-and-through, I really enjoyed my career there.

Bob Dagnall was my first coach as a Saints colts player. I admired him and thought a hell of a lot of him. He was really down to earth and a big help to me. He encouraged me. I played A team for about a year and then I was pushing for first team football. Eric Ashton was coach then and he was really good to me. He held me back for a bit for my own good. I had a lot of admiration for Eric Ashton. Then there was Billy Benyon who made me captain. I thought the world of Billy, his heart and soul was in Saints and he made his players feel the same way. I had some good years with Billy as coach and he was very good to me.

As a younger player when I first got into the side, one of the more experienced players was Tony Karalius. Before a game, Tony always used to be retching and being sick. It ended up making me like that. I was actually sick before every game. It got to the stage where I wouldn't eat before the game. It was just nerves really.

I think the derby games against Wigan stand out for me most, the big crowd and the atmosphere and so on. No matter who we played though, playing for Saints at Knowsley Road was great and I loved it.

I played with a lot of good players during my time at Saints. I had a lot of admiration for George Nicholls, he was like a second dad to me. He really looked after me. Geoff Pimblett stands out for me also. I also think that Bill Francis made me a better player as well. When he came to the club from Wigan I was more a running forward, he certainly put me through some good gaps. Then in later years when I was older and they were younger, I thought Andy Platt was a very good player. Then there was Chris Arkwright, a hard lad and a good player. Graham Liptrot was probably my best mate there, I liked Lippy, he was a good player. There was Neil Holding who did well, the list goes on and on.

I live in Warrington now and I go to St Helens to see my parents who live in Sutton. I don't even watch the game now, not very much anyway. Knowsley Road is Knowsley Road, I used to ride up there before a game to watch the crowds streaming up and it used to get my heart pumping. I'm sure wherever they go though, they'll continue to be successful.

Paul Forber

Paul is from St Helens and made his debut in 1982. He was a popular second-rower for the club in the 1980s and early 1990s. He made a total of 247 appearances for Saints. He was given a testimonial by the club and played in many big games for Saints. He later moved on to play for Salford.

My first game at Knowsley Road was an unbelievable game really. I was a 17-year-old kid and I made my debut in October 1982 against Australia. It was a big game even if I hadn't been a kid and had been playing for a long time. I played against some great players that day, the likes of Wally Lewis, Mal Meninga, Eric Grothe and Wayne Pearce. They brought me on leaps and bounds in just that one game realising how good they were. It's a baptism that you don't really want to have. I was nervous because as a kid walking on the pitch in front of a big crowd that day was really something. That 1982 Australian side was probably the best team that ever came over here. So, they weren't expecting us to do anything special. I remember they beat us 32-0. I thought we'd given a good account of ourselves. We had a lot of young lads playing. As well as me there was Brian Gelling, Gary Bottell, a lot of players who didn't have much first team experience. The team that played us was later rested to be brought back for the first test match against Great Britain at Hull and they won 40-4 so that shows that we hadn't done too badly.

When I was first breaking through into the side, the crowd was brilliant with me. I liked having a go at people and a lot of crowds like seeing you give people a crack. I took a couple and gave a couple out. The crowd responds to things like that and they got behind me. Sometimes, some people thought I was a little bit too daft which I probably was. As time goes on you calm down a little bit but it does take a long time to get it out of your system.

The pitch

Besides Wembley and Old Trafford, Saints' ground is probably the best ground I have ever played on in my life. Saints ground is the same pitch whether you go there in winter or in the middle of summer, it's still like a bowling green. It plays superbly and it's a massive advantage to Saints. Everyone says it looks flat. When you play on there though you find that there is a hill going down towards the restaurant end. You'll notice now that every time Saints win the toss they always play away from the restaurant end in the first half so they can play downhill in the second half. It doesn't look anything at all but when you're on there playing, it makes a massive difference. We used to train on there and of course we got to know every blade of grass on the pitch. That helped a lot.

Big games

I played in a number of big games for the club. I played at Wembley twice which went very quickly both times. I don't remember a lot about it really. We got beaten by Halifax in 1987 when Mark Elia was very unlucky as John Pendlebury knocked the ball out of his hands when he was going in to score right at the end of the game. The other time in 1989 we got annihilated by Wigan which I was very upset about. As a home-town lad, getting beaten by so many was a bit of a disgrace. It was crazy really, we had played Wigan the week before and knocked them out of the Premiership semi-final 4-2 at Wigan when I kicked both goals.

I won the John Player Trophy with the club and played in three Premiership finals. We also had a couple of games where if we had won we had the chance to win the league. Whenever you're playing the big teams like Leeds and Wigan and you have the big crowds there it's special. Especially Wigan, every game against them is like a Wembley. To beat Wigan means so much to the supporters. I have been part of the Saints side that has beaten Wigan on numerous occasions which has always been good.

I enjoyed the big games but it's a lot of the little games that get you to those big games that matter as well. I have been very fortunate to play in quite a few big games for Saints and I have enjoyed every one of them. I do feel sometimes that I haven't performed as I should have in big games. A couple of them I have and a couple of them I haven't. That's possibly down to nerves.

The games at Knowsley Road that stand out most for me are obviously the times where we've beaten Wigan, but perhaps the biggest game for me was playing against New Zealand in October 1989. They'd just beat Australia and they came over here. We were the first game for them on the tour. We must have caught them with a bit of jet lag, they hadn't been beaten for ages. We beat them by one point. Stuart Evans had scored for us then I got the winner. I scored in the corner just by the restaurant. It gave us a great win, I bought every paper the next day because I had made all the headlines which doesn't happen too often. That's the game that sticks out for me.

Part of the opposition

It was brilliant coming back to Saints to play with Salford. Everyone at Saints used to like me and then of course they hated me. When I left Saints I probably played the best rugby I ever played in my life. When I played against Saints I always took it to them. I had come to an agreement with Mike McClennan about leaving the club after 12 years there. We shook hands on it even though I never wanted to leave Saints. I still had two years left on my contract but they thought

70

it was better for me to go. When it comes down to someone not wanting you, then you've got to go. I was pushed away but luckily Salford came in for me and I signed for them. A couple of times when we played Saints at home we annihilated them, once putting the biggest score on them that Salford had recorded since the war. I'll never forget what Mike McClennan said to me after that game. He came up to me, we shook hands and he said: "I think I made a mistake letting you go." Then I just felt like punching him because my heart and soul has always been at Saints. The fans were always good to me.

I've got to say though that Salford was a great move for me, their fans were good as well. I played really well for them and won player of the year a couple of times. I couldn't knock anything about Salford, the chairman John Wilkinson, all the directors, the playing and coaching staff. They were all brilliant with me.

Earlier in my Saints career, I could have gone elsewhere. A couple of teams were interested in me a couple of times. I feel that it doesn't happen with players these days but when I walked out onto the Saints pitch it was my town and I knew everybody there. It was such a privilege to walk out and know that people had come to watch you. You're playing for your home town, your home club. It's a massive achievement, it's everybody's dream who watches Rugby League to play for their home side. The other thing was that it is a massive club as well which spurred me on. The first eight years at Saints I'd have probably played for nothing because I loved playing for the club so much. Then a bit more money came into the game and it got a little bit harder. After 12 years at Saints, like I said I moved to Salford. I could have stayed at Saints forever though. If I had been left alone I'd have still been there now probably.

I only had the one pre-match ritual. About 10 minutes before I went on, I used to be sick until I brought up blood. When I bring up blood, I know I'm all right. It wouldn't matter if I was playing against Australia, Wigan or Runcorn Highfield I would be sick. I had a game for my mate Mark Lee's amateur team Portico against Pilks Recs recently and believe it or not, I was even sick before that. It just must be built into me. It's a bit of nervous energy. I enjoyed having a

Paul Forber (with ball) playing in a charity game at Knowsley Road. Also shown are Paul Loughlin and Shane Cooper.
(Photo: Bernard Platt)

run out with Portico though, even though my ankles are knackered now, it keeps me around the game but not too much involved.

I've not seen many funny things while playing at the ground, you don't seem to get many streakers in Rugby League. The funniest thing was probably at Halifax, I was having a joke with one of their speccies about his missus and he didn't find it too funny. After the game, while I was having my shower the bloke was trying to kick the door down to get at me. The other lads were all laughing in the changing room because this lad had been shouting and chasing me round the pitch.

There's a hell of a lot of history in the Saints ground. There's been some absolutely fantastic players up there. I mean van Vollenhoven and Murphy, I never saw them play but you hear everyone talking about them.

All my friends that I played with like 'Arkie' Chris Arkwright, Neil Holding, Steve Peters, Graham Liptrot, 'Miffer' Johnny Smith, Harry Pinner have had some great games there.

I've played in some great games with them. It's full of memories for me. I go and sit in the restaurant and watch the game, I can close my eyes and open them quickly and recall so many memories from any game.

It's a cracking ground with a tremendous pitch. I think Saints wish they could take the pitch with them. I spent more than 10 years of my life there, they were fantastic years. You had to be good enough to play for Saints and I was lucky enough to do that.

Every player who's played there for the club will all have their own memories. It'll be a funny feeling driving past it when it's not there and there are houses on it.

Phil Veivers

Australian Phil joined Saints alongside Mal Meninga in 1984, originally only intending to stay for six months. That six months became 12 years as Phil made the Saints full-back jersey his own with some superb performances both in defence and attack. Phil made a total of 381 appearances for the club and scored 98 tries. A loyal clubman, who also used to work on the ground, Phil later played for Huddersfield and was on their coaching staff before joining Swinton as a player. Phil is one of the Saints' crowd's favourites to this day and is particularly loved by the Popular side.

The first thing I noticed when I walked onto the Knowsley Road surface was how close the spectators would be and how luscious and well-manicured the pitch looked. The first game I played at Knowsley Road was against Castleford on 7 October 1984. It was a game we won, but I remember after the game people telling me that I hadn't played that well. All that mattered to me was that I'd thought I'd gone all right. I also remember that the previous season in Australia I'd played on the wing so I knew it would take time to adjust.

As I said, it was a great playing surface but the down side of it was always when we got to the end of the season. After the harsh winters and the odd mud bath the dust bowl always appeared in the centre. Also, the Popular side used to freeze up in the middle of winter and make it feel like you were playing on concrete. All-in-all though, it was always a great surface to play on.

In my second game for the club we played a Lancashire Cup semi-final against Leigh at home on a Wednesday night. I remember nearly not playing due to coach Billy Benyon not being impressed with my first game. He'd told me he was going to go with experience and play Steve Rule. My immediate reaction was to ask to speak to him in the back room to explain a few details to him. I also found out later that he didn't even know about me signing for the club and that I wasn't on his agenda. So I told him that I'd come over for a holiday, that I'd come over to meet as many English women as possible and to try as much English beer as possible but that number one, I'd come to play footy. He put me in.

I scored my first try for the club that night. Big Mal put a bomb up on the Leigh full back Chris Johnson, I skipped through, jumped above him, collected it and scored. We progressed through to the final pretty easily that night. Billy came up to me after the game and just said: "I'm glad you've proved me wrong". To this day, we're still close friends and he'll tell you exactly the same story. I've always been a straight shooter and he appreciated that.

Initially when I was going to sign I thought I'd only come over for six months. My family convinced me otherwise and I came for 12. At the back end of that, Saints offered another two- year deal. At the time, I was pretty determined to go back home but after a few phone calls to people I confide in to this day, they convinced me to stay. They said that I could come back over after that contract, and the rest is history.

The fans

The Saints fans were always great, I always had a great rapport with them. The Popular side always tended to have a soft spot for me. Hopefully, throughout my career, I never let them down. I always gave 100 per cent and I think they respected that. They were pretty awesome, in fact it got to the stage where Paul Loughlin and Roy

Haggerty used to say: "Look at him prancing up and down along the touchline, you'd think it was his stand". Whether I was playing or not, those supporters would always come up and talk to me which I'd always reciprocate.

I remember when I first came over I was put up in digs on Lingholme Road with a lovely lady called Mrs Fraser. She asked me one day if I had a pre-match diet so I told her steak, eggs and chips finished off with fruit salad. The first match she cooked for me I came downstairs and there was this massive steak, three eggs and a boatload of chips. I looked at it and thought "you're kidding" but still ploughed through it. Next she said: "I've got your fruit salad". She came out with a massive bowl of fruit salad and I just thought: "I can't eat that". She was a star though, bless her.

I used to have a few superstitions early on in my career, like always eating a Mars Bar before going out to play and wearing two pairs of socks. I always used to stare at my shirt number, number one for four or five minutes before the battle. This just used to focus myself onto the game.

Standout games and players

Playing against touring sides always felt pretty special to me. The Australians with Mal, Gene Miles and the legends was special. Beating the Kiwis in 1989 was fantastic. Beating any touring side is special, like the time we beat Auckland 52-26 in November 1987.

Other games that stick in the mind are beating Wigan 41-6 the day after Boxing Day 1992. They scored first and never came close again. Other stand outs are the night Shane Cooper scored six tries against Hull in February 1988 and the day we put the century past Carlisle in 1986.

I played with a number of star quality players at Saints. The likes of Harry Pinner, fantastic with the ball in his hands but I had to do his tackling as well as Graham Liptrot's (joking) who also was great with the ball in his hands. And those hard men like Roy Haggerty and Chris Arkwright. Roy always had a knack of getting out a great one-armed offload. Arkie was tough but knew how to play footy.

Phil Veivers (Photo: Bernard Platt)

Barrie Ledger could finish from anywhere. No-one's probably mentioned Sean Day, whether he could play or not didn't matter because he could kick goals. Paul Loughlin was another great player, I don't think he got the rub of the green with the fans though. His record speaks for itself with the amount of points he scored for the club and the number of international caps he gained. He was a real winger's centre.

Another tough cookie was Bernard 'Barney' Dwyer. He was a real grafter, we always had secret battles in training and when we played. Both Locks [Loughlin] and Barney are still close friends.

Towards the back end of my time there, Keiron Cunningham was arriving on the scene and Gary Connolly had been and gone with the fans calling him 'Judas'. I think I told him to go in the end. I have to say though that all the guys who've pulled on the red and white shirt have done a great job over the years. I've seen many come and go as well as coaches. Saints always had a great side with limited finances but Wigan always had the money to go out and buy the superstars.

Opposition players who've stuck in my mind over the years are Shaun Edwards who was a great competitor as was Ellery Hanley. There were also Alan Rathbone and Les Boyd who were tough guys.

76

Garry 'cod eyes' Schofield and John Woods were skilful players. Andy Gregory made Wigan and Andy Farrell is doing just the same now. Lee Crooks was a great ball-playing prop, but there was none better than Kevin 'Fred' Ward whom I played with and against. There was no better prop in the game than 'Fred' at that time.

As for coaches at Saints, I enjoyed my time under Billy Benyon. He definitely got our fitness levels up and came up with two trophies then got the bullet. Mike McClennan was very shrewd and very tactical. He was a great bloke but mention 'footy' and he started to sweat and get pumped up. He was a bundle of nerves coming into a game. He actually provided the strangest thing I've seen at Knowsley Road. That was the ploy where big John Harrison headed the ball over the line for George Mann to score. It was outlawed after that.

One of the funniest things I saw at the ground involves Lockers. We used to work on the ground and were forever playing pranks on each other. It was his turn to make the brew this day and he was scared of rats. So we put a dead rat in the coffee jar. To see his face as the jar smashed and he took off across the pitch was hilarious.

In 1996, the board in their wisdom decided it was time for me to vacate Knowsley Road. I'd heard the whisper from upstairs that I couldn't be selected again or they wouldn't be able to get rid of me because I'd be part of the team. The straw that broke the camel's back was when we went to Wembley and I wasn't picked after playing in every round that year. They went onto win, after three loser's medals I thought I had a chance. Anyway, *que sera sera.*

It would have been nice to have been part of the coaching staff but it wasn't to be. At the time I was departing, I thought it would have made perfect sense to put me in charge of the A team to bring on the youngsters and to increase stability within the club.

Since I've left I was invited back to Knowsley Road to do the half-time draw. The old Popular side kicked in again to make me feel very welcome.

Bobbie Goulding

Bobbie joined the club from Widnes in 1994. Within a short space of time he became captain of the side. His play-making and kicking abilities from scrum-half made him one of the most influential players in the club's recent history. His skills and personality quickly made him an idol among the fans at Knowsley Road. Bobbie made 155 appearances for the club kicking 548 goals. He led the team to two Challenge Cup wins in 1996 and 1997 with his tactical kicking proving crucial in both games. He also lifted the inaugural Super League title in front of more than 18,000 fans at Knowsley Road in 1996 before leaving in 1998. He now plays for Salford.

I didn't really gain any initial impression of the ground, but I got a feeling that the time is right for me to be here at this club. It was a feeling I've never had before and I don't think I'll ever have again. I knew something special was going to happen and it did. It looked a good professional club to come to.

I'd played there many times for other clubs and it's always been one of the best surfaces in Rugby League.

My first game for Saints at the ground was a match against Doncaster in 1994. The speccies were behind us from the word go. Apollo Perelini had signed, Scott Gibbs had signed and I'd signed. Three big names coming to the club, two from Union and one from Rugby League. Coming out, the atmosphere was great. I can still remember running out. It's a good place for atmosphere even when you've only got 6 or 7,000 there.

My relationship with the Saints fans was something else. I've never known a relationship like it before with any sportsman and I don't think you ever will see one again to be truthful. It summed it up for me in an early game in my Saints career when we played Castleford at Knowsley Road in September 1994. We won 47-14 and I had a great game. I think it's the best game I've ever played in my life. Every time I touched the ball, something happened. Either there was a try, I put someone through a gap or put a good kick to touch in. I didn't want the game to stop. I couldn't get tired. We were winning convincingly and I kicked a goal from the touchline. I was walking back and a spectator ran on the field. I didn't know what he was running on for. Was he a Castleford fan? I thought hang on a minute, what is he going to do? He got down in front of me and he bowed to me. That was probably my best individual moment at Saints.

Ten minutes after that, I kicked the ball to the corner for Alan Hunte to score. I kicked the goal from the touchline. As I ran back I repaid the compliment by getting down on my knees in front of the halfway line.

Lifting trophies

Winning twice at Wembley with Saints was brilliant, probably the second best feeling in my life following my kids being born. It was also a big relief because I knew the way things were between Wigan and Saints from my time at Wigan. When I came to Saints, the big thing was taking what was termed as Wigan's cup off them. For the Saints speccies, it just must have been a feeling of relief.

I sat in the bath after that first Wembley win and just let out a huge sigh of relief because I knew we'd done something. I had such an emotional feeling as my son Bob came up the steps with me, it was the best feeling in the world. He was always going to be there. I always knew we were going to beat Bradford that day. Even when we were 26-12 behind I knew we would win the trophy. No matter if they had scored 50 points, we were still going to win the cup. Somebody upstairs had looked down on me and said make sure Bob is at the top of the steps because you will win the cup.

Then of course, there was the day we won the Super League title on the last day of the season in 1996 at home to Warrington. Alex Murphy was coach at Warrington along with John Dorahy. I remember being on Sky TV after the match and they asked me: "Are you going to party now?" I said "yes, nobody was going to stop us, not even Alex Murphy". He was a great for Saints from years ago and it's been a privilege to meet Murph on the way around and to be classed in the same category as him is fabulous. Winning the first Super League, especially winning it at Knowsley Road on the last day of the season was superb. The last four games of the season were Castleford, Paris, Sheffield and Warrington and we had to win all four because Wigan were within a point of us. We knew we were going to do it though. You take incidents from the games like when Steve Prescott made that great tackle on Jason Flowers at Castleford. You knew it was going to be our year. We all hung in for one another, we all died for one another. We all knew that it was going to be our season and no-one was going to stop it. Lifting that trophy at Knowsley Road in front of our supporters was magnificent. Just to see the relief on the supporter's faces was tremendous. The faces said it all, we've won this off Wigan as well. It was a great achievement. The expression on people's faces that day, no-one can ever take that away from me, I've got that.

When I first started playing for Wigan, that was a great side. You just name the names, Edwards, Hanley, Gregory, Bell, the two Iros and Goodway. You go through the whole side and that was just a brilliant side to play in. As a kid coming through you just looked around in awe really. Having said that though, the Saints side of 1996 was right up there with it. We needed to add a couple of players. If we had done that we would have surpassed that great Wigan side. We never added them and we lost players in fact. If you asked me to name a dream team of all the players I've played alongside, there would be five or six members of that Saints side in 1996. That includes all the Great Britain sides I've played in as well. Looking at the side in my first season at Saints, you had Shane Cooper. I feel that Shane should still be at Saints in some capacity. He did so much for the club in the years he was there. He was brilliant and good to be about. We had a good side that first season but it was one of those Saints sides where we would score 40 and let the opposition score 30. You can't do that, you've got to put sides to bed. That was our downfall. I mean, we went to Wigan in February 1995 and drew 16-16 with them in the Challenge Cup where I hit the post with a drop goal. We came back to Knowsley Road in midweek with high expectations in front of 17,000 and they beat us comfortably. I'm glad it didn't happen until 1996 though because I was captain then and I went up for the cup. Things always happen for a reason.

Another game that stands out for me is when we beat Wigan in the cup in February 1997 when I got sent off. That was still a good result for me as captain.

Intimidating

Knowsley Road is an intimidating ground to come to as an opposing player. I remember playing there with Widnes in 1993. It was a night match with the floodlights on and it was intimidating when the Saints crowd started really getting on our backs. I've always found, though, that if a side is getting hammered by Saints from the word go then the speccies are bad to the opposition and they keep going.

If you're in a tight game with Saints and you keep with them, come the last 15 or 20 minutes the Saints speccies start panicking and they get on the Saints' players backs. I think that's why Wigan always beat Saints at Saints. A lot of teams have said: "Let's keep in with them because come the last 20 minutes the crowd will start to have a go at Saints". Coaches like Phil Larder, John Monie and Dougie Laughton have always said that if you keep in with Saints, you've got a chance.

I have quite a few pre-match rituals. I always wear a ring with a cross on that my granddad gave me before he died. I always pray half an hour before we go out. I have pictures of my kids with me which I put up on my peg in the dressing room. I also have little motivational messages which I take with me. As I make my way onto the field, I always make the sign of the cross and look up to the sky. Then it's time for work.

The feeling when you play Wigan and you lead your side out as captain at Knowsley Road is indescribable. The hairs on the back of your neck stand up, and you get a cramp down your neck. The new tunnel under the main stand at Saints isn't as good as the old one. The new one is wide and everyone can just get out onto the pitch. The old one was narrow, you came up it and once you ran out you're on your own. When you were coming through that old tunnel, you could hear the noise building and then it would hit you. It's electric, you get butterflies in your stomach. It was an amazing place when the speccies were up for it. When they are, there is no better place in Rugby League for atmosphere because it's a compact ground and the speccies seem to be right on top of you.

Someone I played with at Saints who stands out for me is Shane Cooper. He was a good leader and taught me quite a bit even though we were only together in the side for about eight months. His attitude to training was first class. Another one would have to be Keiron Cunningham who is a good friend of mine. When Keiron was first coming through we drew 16-16 with Wigan in the Cup. Eric Hughes, coach at the time, had a problem. He didn't know whether to play Sean Casey, Bernard Dwyer or Phil Veivers at hooker that day. I said to him: "I'd put young Keiron Cunningham in". Eric Hughes looked at me as if to say "you're joking". I said: "No, put him in, he'll do us well". Keiron took the man of the match in that game and he never looked back. You can look at every player I played with at the club really. You look at Scott Gibbs, every time he got the ball the crowd would rise. When that happens, you know you've got something. He was a robust runner who did well. I played with a lot of special players in that time.

Bobbie Goulding at Knowsley Road celebrating
the 1997 Challenge Cup victory (Photo: Bernard Platt)

Wembley 1996: Bobbie Goulding and Keiron Cunningham celebrate
Saints' victory (Photo: Bernard Platt)

I will get something from Knowsley Road that will go in the barn
I am doing up which will have memorabilia and a pool table and
things like that in. What I get from the ground will be centre-spot for
me in there. It will be sad because three of my kids were born while I
was at Saints. There was Bob, then Bradley, then Ellie. I felt like
Saints was my home, thought that I was invincible that they would
never get rid of me. The place brings back a lot of good memories for
me. I wouldn't say any bad memories. I left the club under a cloud
but when I left I never slagged anybody off. I left, I knew what it was
for, I held my hand up. I'll always look at Knowsley Road as the
place where I had the best rugby I ever had in my life - the happiest
times anyway. I went there and people were saying: "If they can get
him to play and do things properly", I had four years when I did do
everything properly. There were some bad things but we're not all
"saints". I enjoyed all my time there except the last few months
which was a bit hard, when they took the captaincy off me but I'll

hold my hands up and say it was my fault. My relationship with the Saints fans was unique. For me, St Helens is the best club anyone could ever play for, the best.

Shaun McRae

Shaun McRae joined Saints as head coach in 1996 after spending more than a decade as assistant coach at top Australian club Canberra Raiders. He coached St Helens for three very successful years. The side won the Challenge Cup for the first time in 20 years in 1996, they added the first Super League title later that year giving the club its first double for 30 years and followed it up with another Wembley success in 1997. This was the first time in the club's history that Saints had won back to back Challenge Cups. Shaun is currently coach of Super League side Hull FC.

When first approached to take the coaching job at Saints I felt very humbled really. To be considered worthy enough of such a fine establishment as St Helens, a club that has such a great history in the game of Rugby League, such a big strong, powerful club with a great name, not just in the UK but in the world, I felt very honoured. I thoroughly enjoyed the three years I was there. I think it's fair to say you feel the pressure straight away.

Welcome to Britain: Shaun McRae in the snow at Knowsley Road
(Photo: Bernard Platt)

84

Saints were a club that was perhaps considered the bridesmaids rather than the bride. There were a lot of challenges there for me. I know they'd won things in the past but they hadn't won anything for quite a long time.

It was my first job as head coach after being assistant coach with Canberra for a long time. I'd also been on the coaching staff with the Australian and New Zealand test sides but Saints was my first head coaching role and it was a great place to start. I still feel very honoured. I've got great memories of St Helens, the people, the players I worked with and, of course, the ground itself is a tremendous Rugby League ground.

First impressions

My first impressions of Knowsley Road were the great atmosphere and terrific playing surface. The groundsman at the time was Neil Holding and he did a wonderful job while I was there. It was always a great place to play, I used to say to opposition players that I knew that: "it's a pleasure to make a tackle or be tackled on this surface". It's everything you would imagine when you live in Australia and see English grounds on TV. It reminded me of when I was watching English games in Australia. The houses around the ground, just the surroundings and also the atmosphere that was created there by the supporters. They were parochial and patriotic, it was tremendous when it was near capacity.

My first game at Knowsley Road was when we beat Wigan 41-26 in April 1996. It's an expression that I use a lot when I talk to people about St Helens or do public speaking or anything, is the old 'chestpoke'. You get the poke in the chest accompanied with: "Just beat Wigan, we don't care if we lose every other game, just beat Wigan". To come out in that game and win we had to play really well that day. It was a special occasion because it's such a huge crowd, and there's a lot of pressure to face Wigan because it's the traditional local derby. It's a rivalry I had trouble coming to terms with when I was first at the club. Believe me, now I understand!

There were more than 15,000 in the ground that day. We were under a lot of pressure because we had already qualified for Wembley whilst Wigan had bowed out to Salford and the league and Premiership were the only things they had to play for. My first memories were it probably doesn't get any better than this but of course it did. It was a great victory and it made me realise how much it meant to the fans, not only to beat Wigan but to play well and win games. I saw the elation on the players' faces after the game as well.

Everybody wants to win and I think at a club like St Helens you're under pressure to win all the time. That can sometimes be unfair but it's something that's been created at the club, it's nobody's fault, that's just history and the result of being a successful club. There are plenty of other clubs in the same position. It was a great way to launch our league campaign at home.

Big games

As for the games that stand out for me during my three years, that first one against Wigan is one. The last game in 1996 when we beat Warrington to clinch the title was also important. It was 66-14. It was a Bank Holiday Monday on 26 August 1996 and we had the pressure of already having won the cup that year and having to back up after that. We were a point behind Wigan in the table and we had to win that game to win the first ever Super League. Tommy Martyn scored from the first set of six from a kick. That really launched us into the game. We played some unbelievable rugby that day and there were more than 18,000 in the ground. It was a fantastic day.

There are so many games that are difficult to recall though, we had a tremendous home record in those three years. I know there was the bad loss to Wigan when we had a lot of injuries and the World Club Championship where we didn't do as well as I thought we might but no English club did, that wasn't just us. I still thought we played well in some of those games. I remember the last play-off game at home in October 1998 against Bradford as well because of the wonderful send-off I was given. We won comfortably but I recall being able to go on the field after the game and in my way say thank you to everyone and obviously accept the plaudits of the supporters. I have to say that during the three years I was there I was very well received and I have been since I've gone back. I'm very grateful for that because sometimes I see people from other clubs return to places they were once at and not get received in the way they probably should. That's something I'm very grateful to the St Helens public for, I made a lot of friends and acquaintances there and I still have them now. People are not silly and I think they have an understanding of what goes on at clubs. The three years were good and it would have been nice to have been there a bit longer. That Bradford game stands out because it was my last home game coaching at such a historic club.

There was also the cup win at home to Wigan in February 1997 when we won with 12 men after Bobbie Goulding was sent from the field. That was a fantastic victory.

Against clubs like Warrington, Castleford, Halifax and Sheffield, we always seemed to rattle up a big score at home. They just couldn't get close to us. It was a bit of a different story when we were away although Warrington never beat us while I was at St Helens.

Playing and coaching staff

I was just happy to have worked with some tremendously talented athletes, some wonderful players, excellent coaching staff such as Mike Gregory, people like Nigel Ashley-Jones, people like Jeanette Smith, Stan Wall and many, many others. There was Brian Case whom I worked with very closely with regards the alliance side for two years. There was also Nick Halafihi who was in charge of development and the academy side. I apologise if I leave anyone out but I can't name everybody. Guys like Brian Collins who was very supportive, almost took on a sort of fatherly role and he did my stats while I was there. He was a tremendous help to me. These were people who were supportive all the time, whether you won or you lost, that's what you want. It's all right to share the emotions of the successes and the wins but it's the losing where you want people to support you. I think that's where you find out your true characters and your true friends and not fair-weather people who always want to be around you when you're winning. The people I respect are the ones that support you when you're going through rough patches. Some of the people I mentioned there plus others were very good.

There was a tremendous chairman in Eric Ashton, but I've got to say the guy who really had a tremendous influence on the club, I enjoyed working with him and I'm still very good friends with is David Howes. St Helens now are still successful but I think a lot of that is based on what David did in those years at the club. To me, David Howes is one of the best administrators in the game and certainly one of the most professional people I've ever worked with and a tremendous character as well. I was very disappointed to see him leave the club but it wasn't much longer after that I left anyway. Those are the things that happen.

As for the players who stand out for me during my time at Saints, again I can't mention everybody and apologise to anyone I miss out, it isn't deliberate.

One of the smartest players I ever coached at Saints was Scott Gibbs. I say that even though I know he didn't play a lot of games for us when I was there and I was really disappointed when he went back to Rugby Union. I saw a lot of improvement in the two Samoans, Apollo Perelini and Vila Matautia. When I first took over that club, I saw some talent that I thought could improve immensely. I felt there were a few discipline problems. I felt there were a few skills that were lacking and the conditioning process wasn't good enough. Their mental approach to games wasn't good enough. There were a lot of things to improve on. Those three players were among the biggest improvers. I was really disappointed when we lost Gibbs because I thought given time we could have had a champion player on our hands. Then there's the professionalism of guys like Anthony Sullivan, Chris Joynt even Bobbie Goulding when it came to training and playing on the field, all class players.

To me, and I still say this now, the best player at the club is Tommy Martyn. He is the key player. Whenever we had Tommy Martyn playing, we never seemed to lose. And there was an outstanding hooker in Keiron Cunningham, he was only 19 or 20 when I worked with him and he's just going to get better. He always had the mark of a champion. Later on, there was Paul Sculthorpe, I think he's proved his value, and the brilliance of a Paul Newlove who could get you out of trouble, as damaging a centre as I have ever seen in my life, a guy that could score out of nothing which is so difficult to stop. Then we had unsung heroes like Julian O'Neill who worked really hard and I'm surprised Saints let him go. I thought the signing of Sean Long was tremendous. I've got to say, both David Howes and myself worked very hard to get him at the club. I'm delighted to see how his career has blossomed because there was a lot of negativity towards him from certain factions within the club. It's a tremendous thing for Sean and he's a brilliant athlete. I thought we got a lot out of Derek McVey, he was probably in the twilight of his career but he still did very well for us.

There are so many outstanding players who came through the club, so again I apologise to those I left out. The secret of St Helens is that they've got so many outstanding players. They have key players and match winners all over the park. That's the reason they put so many points on teams. Saints might let in 20 or 24 points but you've got to score 40 or 50 to beat them at times. That's a difficult thing to achieve.

For all those players, there's obviously been some disappointments, players who showed a lot of potential but never quite achieved what they were capable of. It would be unfair of me to mention names. It's all right talking about players doing this, doing that but there have been instances when you would have liked to get more out of some of the others.

Wembley at the double

The two Wembley cup finals were unbelievable experiences, not just the game but the whole weekend and the aftermath of the games. Having won both games makes it a lot easier to talk about. In the first final in 1996 against Bradford, it was a win against all odds. We were down 26-12 with not long remaining and the way we came back was a credit to the players. They hung in there and believed that they could do it. It was wonderful to come back into the town and be so well received. I can remember going to the town hall and the weather was pretty poor that afternoon.

After winning the following year in 1997 we went back to Knowsley Road and it was far better weather wise. I always felt I was more comfortable about winning it the second year. I always felt that we would have learnt a lot from the year before. Bradford probably felt the same because they'd been there and lost. The old saying is sometimes you need to lose a big game to win one. The second final was probably better in that respect. I just felt we were a lot more composed and confident in the 1997 final. The 1996 game, we were a little bit disjointed, trying to show too much flair and flamboyance. I don't think that always works in major finals. However, the one thing you'll never take out of the St Helens team and I don't think any coach will ever manage it, is to take away the flair and flamboyance. That's why you need to take some blood pressure tablets sometimes. They were great victories and the players learnt a lot from them. There are still players playing today who have those winner's medals and that's something that can never be taken away from them.

To be part of bringing that long-awaited success to the club and to have a good team with you on and off the field, I thought was absolutely wonderful. They are memories I'll always cherish and I'll always try to remember until I suffer from senile dementia or something. It's nice to have been part of the history of the club.

The strangest thing that happened to me at the club and I must point out that I don't mean to be disrespectful to anybody at all, was one of my first training sessions. You used to come out of the old changing rooms which are under the old board room. You used to come down the tunnel to go out onto the field. But the gate was shut, I had the team behind me so I opened the gate and there was someone standing at the gate who said: "I'm sorry, you can't go out there." I replied: "Of course we can go out there, we've got a practice session, it's the last day before a game, we're ready to go." He said: "No, you can't come out." I asked him why not and he said:

"Well, someone's having their ashes scattered across the field." I didn't believe it, I'd never heard of it before, so I said: "No, you're joking". So I started walking out there and of course there's the ceremony in the middle of the pitch so I was a bit embarrassed. I didn't go all the way out and so the ceremony wasn't interrupted fortunately. When I consulted some people afterwards, they said it was quite common for people to do that. I don't mean to be disrespectful but it was quite funny at the time because I'd never heard of such a thing before. I think the players knew but wouldn't say anything because they knew I wouldn't have believed them.

I understand the need for new stadia in the game and I understand the need to progress. You can't stand still. This new ground venture has been spoken about since I was at the club and probably before. There's a part of everybody in a ground. There's a part of people's emotions, heart and soul in a place. I think the most important thing is for the club to exist.

I know history is wonderful and people will say: "Knowsley Road was the only place to watch St Helens". I can understand that emotion because most things are based on emotion. There have been decisions made and people become emotional. I think a person's real heart and soul is in the club wherever the club is. As long as it's in St Helens that's the place for it to be. There have been some wonderful pitter-patters of little feet and big feet playing on that ground. There have been some wonderful athletes and wonderful memories for everyone to have enjoyed and lived through. There have probably been some sad times and difficult times as well. At the end of the day though, Knowsley Road will be almost like a shrine in terms of Rugby League. Just because it won't be there doesn't mean that the club won't exist. I think the most important thing is that the club exists and that people continue to support St Helens Rugby League club, no matter where they are.

Keiron Cunningham

Keiron broke into the first team in 1994 and made his home debut in early 1995. Playing for his home-town club, Keiron has now established himself as the Great Britain hooker. Indeed he is often described as "the best number nine in the world" impressing the Australians whenever he has played against them with his powerful running style and hard-hitting defence. During his time at Saints, Keiron has won three Challenge Cups, three Super League titles and a World Club Championship.

My first game in the first team at Knowsley Road was against Hull in January 1995. It was obviously very memorable, I remember it being very physical and fast. It's difficult to explain the difference between the alliance and the first team. It was an honour to do it, being a local lad and playing for your home town. I remember feeling shattered, glad to get through it and just waiting to see what was round the corner.

Rugby League has always been my life, my brothers had played, there is a very big rugby background in my family. There was a lot of pressure on me with people saying: "you're gonna make it" but you don't know that. I mean, how many young lads have been told they were going to make it only for them to be digging roads now. Pulling on that shirt for the first team was a real honour. I've never regretted it and never will. I've never looked back from doing it.

The supporters treated me really well when I broke into the team. I think I'd played three away games, then I got dropped and then I came back for my first home game. I had a decent game and they took to me well. It was tough to come into the Saints first team because all the Saints fans adored current hooker Bernard Dwyer. Bernard was a great servant to the club, a brilliant player and he's a good friend. For me as a young lad coming through it was very difficult being in Bernard's shadow. The fans accepted it brilliantly though. I get a lot of support from them. I started off at full-back, then played at scrum-half, I think I'm the only player to play in every

A young Keiron Cunningham. (Photo: Bernard Platt)

position, although I actually signed for the club as a hooker. What you find sometimes though is people who sign for the club in a certain position end up being moulded into another position when they get into the first team. Look at Paul Wellens, he was a stand-off, yet now he's one of the finest full-backs in the country. I fitted into the role of hooker when I was about 15.

Knowsley Road is brilliant to play on. For me, it's the best stadium in the world. I love it, I love the atmosphere especially when you've got a full house there. The fans are one of the best sets of supporters in the league. It's a lovely stadium and I'm really going to miss it when it goes. For the young lads coming through now, perhaps Knowsley Road doesn't mean as much to them. To me, I've grown up with it and Knowsley Road is my home ground. Everyone enjoys playing at home and I think the same goes for every side.

I don't really have any pre-match rituals. If it's a night time game I tend to stay in bed all day, get as much sleep as possible and eat as much as I can. I always shave my hair in a morning as well.

It's phenomenal running onto the pitch for one of the big games at Knowsley Road - indescribable. You get a tingle from your feet to your head. It's an amazing feeling. I class the big games at home, the likes of Bradford and Wigan in the same bracket as playing for Great Britain or walking out at Old Trafford for the Grand Final. You've got more pride at Knowsley Road because it's your home ground.

I don't really take "the world's best number nine" tag in. I'm a down-to-earth person who gets on with everybody as any spectator will tell you. To me, it's just a tag that you carry round with you. One day someone is going to take the tag off me. I would openly admit that I think I am the best hooker in Great Britain. On a world-wide stage, I perform when I play for Great Britain and perform really well. I think I'd have to go to Australia and play in the NRL before I could hold my hands up and say: "I am the best in the world". Whether that's being modest I don't know. I'd like to go out there and play week-in, week-out because it's a tough competition, obviously I wouldn't get as many opportunities as I do over here. Unless I did that, I couldn't really say.

Winning the cup

It was absolutely brilliant bringing the Challenge Cup back to St Helens in 1996 and 1997. I think 1996 was the more special of the two as we were underdogs, we were never going to win and 1996 was the first time I'd been to Wembley - I mean I'd been as a kid watching Saints but this was my first time playing. It was great to walk out on the turf. No-one gave us a hope in hell of beating Bradford. It was the same in 1997 when Bradford were dominating the league. They were
beating sides with huge scores. But 1996 sticks out in my mind as the sweetest though because it was the first one although 1997 was good because after the game I took my daughter onto the field with me. We've got some great pictures and it's nice when you can involve

your family in a day like that. Those are memories that are great to look back on. Coming back, I did have a big hangover as well which didn't help. We did have a good drinking session after the game as you can probably imagine.

Hopefully during my career at Saints we can win the Cup again [achieved in April 2001]. It always seems to suit Saints to be underdogs, we don't like to be favourites, that seems to be more pressure than we can handle possibly. We like going into a game where people say we've got no chance and we go in and kick them up the arse and say: "Get that into you". That's how good Saints can be.

1996 title decider

I was so nervous before the title decider against Warrington in 1996 it was untrue. Normally, if you play on a Sunday, it's on a Wednesday that you start to feel nervous, because that's the day you recover from
the knocks you took in the previous game and you start preparing for the next.

For the Wire game though, I was nervous from as soon as the hooter went at the end of the previous game which was Sheffield at home. We'd beat them convincingly 68-2 and going home I was thinking about the Warrington game.

For me, winning the league is one of my biggest achievements. I do believe that if you finish top of the league you should receive something for it. I know you get rewarded for that by the fact that you only have to win one game to get to the Grand Final but even so you should get some sort of acknowledgement for it.

Winning the league was one of the biggest highlights of my career so far definitely. We were awesome in that Warrington game, untouchable. We've got a great side now but it's a much closer competition. In 1996 we seemed to be head and shoulders above the rest. When we'd played Warrington at Wilderspool earlier in the season, it had been a really close game with Ian Pickavance going in for the winning try before Warrington missed a late penalty goal that

Keiron Cunningham receiving the 2000 fanzine Player of the Year award.
(Photo: Andrew Quirke)

would have given them the game. I was so nervous. They had loads of players out, there was loads of stuff in the papers. Alex Murphy was their coach then and he was saying he's not going to do this and that because it's St Helens.

During the game, there was an incident that really typified our spirit. Warrington's Richard Henare was going over the line for a try and Sully ran back and knocked the ball out of his hands. We really wanted it and there was no doubt in our mind that we were going to win that game. We had great team spirit. The only thing I'm upset about is that in all the pictures they took when the side was posing with the trophy I seem to have someone standing in front of me or Bobbie Goulding's arm covering my face. I've got the medal but I haven't got the memorabilia. Someone will have a picture somewhere so I'm sure one will turn up eventually.

Two other games that stand out for me are the Warrington games in the centenary season in 1995. We played them twice in a week. We had a midweek game in the semi-final of the Regal Trophy where we beat them 80-0. Then on the Sunday in the league we beat them easily again 54-14. Those two games really stand out for me, don't ask me why. We really performed well in both games. I scored a good try as well in the second game. I got the ball on my own 20 yard line and ran, there was no-one in front of me so I kept going. Obviously the great victories over Wigan or when you play well against Bradford, those matches stand out for you.

I owe Eric Hughes a lot. Eric gave me my chance. I don't think he's ever regretted giving me my chance either. You can't really compare coaches because they all coach in their own way. Ian Millward is a great coach, he's absolutely brilliant. Shaun McRae is a brilliant coach. Ian Millward lacks some things that Shaun McRae has and Shaun McRae lacks some things that Ian Millward has. The perfect coach would be if you could take a piece from each one of them. If you could have Ellery Hanley's discipline, Shaun McRae's technical expertise, Ian Millward's knowledge of the game and Eric Hughes's will to win then you'd have the perfect coach. In their own right, they're all great coaches. I don't think any of them will ever be out of a job.

I think the strangest thing I've seen at the ground is some of the pre-match entertainment they have. They come out with some crackers, I don't know where they get them from. You also hear some funny things coming from the touchline sometimes, you know people effing and jeffing at the touch judge or referee. That brings a giggle sometimes. Most of the time, you're so focused on the game you don't really notice anything else.

Future

I'd like to achieve as much as I can in the game, I'd like to continue playing for Great Britain. One day I'd like to captain Saints, that's a big ambition of mine. Whether it comes off or not, I don't know but hopefully it will. I'd like Saints to be successful. I've been lucky, I've come through, we've had a great side and Saints have won lots of trophies. Hopefully, during my time at Saints, we can win more cups. Any Rugby League player wants to win as many medals as they can. I'd like Saints to be consistent and keep up what they've done recently and win things: beat Wigan, beat Bradford, be known as a very successful side. Long term, I'd like to go into coaching but that's a long way down the track.

I'd like to finish my career at Saints. I had a big decision to make in 1999 when my contract was due to run out in 2000. I had an offer from Wigan to sign for them when I came out of contract at Saints which I turned down. I had offers from Australia from when I went over there to play for Great Britain at the end of 1999. It was very tempting and I'd love to play out there but I think if I was going to go 1999 would have been the time to make the move. I've got another three seasons on my current deal, who knows what will happen during that time? Who knows what's round the corner? Saints might not offer me another deal or someone from Australia might come in for me, you don't know. At the end of the day, I've got a family, a house and kids to feed so that's my number one priority. In an ideal world though, I'd love to finish my career at Saints. Hopefully, when my current deal is close to running out, we can extend it with a view to me finishing my playing days at the club.

The new stadium to me is going to be like an away ground. Look at Wigan, when they first moved it was hard for them. You're performing like you're playing away. Over time you get used to it and you define it as your home ground. Having said that, it's not the same and I don't think anything will be the same as Knowsley Road. The close proximity of the fans at the ground is something you can't recreate in a new stadium.

It's the best playing surface in the game along with Headingley. The ground has always been good but they've been lucky as the area is all sandstone. It's a great foundation for the pitch. There's a couple of younger lads at the club who are talking about buying houses on it when they put them up on Knowsley Road.

Chris Joynt

Signed from Oldham in September 1992, Chris soon made his mark in the St Helens side as a quick, strong-running, try-scoring second row forward. Five years after signing for the club and after picking up a Super League winners medal and two Challenge Cup winners medals, Ireland and Great Britain international Chris was named captain of the Saints side, a position he holds to this day. Christened "Captain Fantastic" by the supporters, Chris leads by example and has led his side to two Grand Final wins and a World Club Challenge victory over Brisbane as well as the treble-clinching 2001 Challenge Cup final win over Bradford. Chris scored two tries against Wigan in the 2000 Grand Final and a crucial try against Brisbane in the WCC. Twice a Harry Sunderland Award winner and one of the most consistent players at the club, Chris has scored more than 100 tries and is well on his way to making 300 appearances.

The reason I came to play for Saints was because when I was at Oldham we played Saints in the Challenge Cup at the Watersheddings and I had a half-decent game. The next thing that happened was Saints were knocking on my door and I moved to the club in 1992.

When I came into the club you had to admire the likes of Shane Cooper, Paul Loughlin, Kevin Ward, Tea Ropati and George Mann, who were really good players in the game. With regard to the present day, it's good playing alongside Newy, Tommy and Anthony Sullivan who I've spent six or seven years of my career with. Tommy's taken the same path as me, he played at Oldham with me when we were first coming into the game. He signed for Saints not long after I did.

The coach when I arrived here was Mike McClennan, a New Zealander who I had a lot of respect for. He gave me my first chance in the big league. He was a great coach and at that time the game was part-time. We used to meet on Tuesday and Thursday to train and then play on the Sunday. He was a top bloke, a good coach. Next up was Eric Hughes, Eric was very keen on discipline. Again, we had a good side and one great thing about Eric was that he would bring the youth through the club and that provided dividends in 1996 and 1997 when Shaun McRae took over. The team was ready for winning things because we had a great blend of youth and experience which

Eric had left. Shaun McRae brought a whole new meaning to the game, we had gone full-time, we were in a new era, and you could spend a lot more time on analysing your game. Shaun brought a whole new dimension into the game. Then came Ellery and I must say he was my favourite player as a youngster. His game-plans were so simple but so effective which was proved by us winning Super League IV. With me being a player who had admired him when he played, if he says you can do it, you could do it. He had coached me previously with Great Britain in 1994 and he's a top chap. Onto the present day with Ian Millward and he has made us all appreciate being a League player. It is hard work and he doesn't mind us enjoying ourselves if we achieve as long as we have no injuries. He's a very technical coach. You can't help but learn off the fella. I can honestly say that I've learned something from all the coaches I've had and I respect them all.

Knowsley Road is arguably the best surface in the competition. Although with the introduction of the [football] Liverpool Reserves on it over the past couple of years and more so this year with St Helens Town as well, combined with a bad winter, the pitch is showing some signs of wear and tear but overall it is still a fantastic surface.

My relationship with the Saints fans is one of respect. I respect them, they respect me. They cannot knock anybody who gives 100 per cent week-in, week-out even if the results don't go our way. There's nothing more pleasing as a player than seeing spectators who travel to away games.

It's a fantastic honour to captain such a great club, the lads are very professional and it's an honoured job. The day I don't think I can handle the job I will gladly hand it down to somebody who can but at this moment in time I can fill the post without a problem. At the end of the day, I captain the side but I'm just one of the team. The first thing I think when I'm leading the team out is to get my own game in order and to lead by example because actions speak louder than words.

When I lead the side out, you'll see that I throw something to one side and that's to do with my gumshield. After the previous game, the gumshield sort of sets like concrete in its case. What I do is put my gumshield in a cup of warm water and that then softens the gumshield. When I enter the pitch I throw away the cup with warm water in it.

On game day, I tend to get up at the same time and it's more of a routine than superstition. One of the great games I can recall that I took part in at Knowsley Road is the Lancashire Cup Final in the 1992-93 season against Wigan when we lost 5-4. That was a great game. At that time, myself and Jason Robinson were both up-and-coming young players in the game. *League Express* gave myself and Jason man-of-the-match which was a massive achievement at that time. Also, the 41-6 drubbing of Wigan in 1992, the one thing that sticks in my mind was that we were sponsored by Coors Lager for the day and wore their logo on the shirt. We got to keep the shirts and what a great win that was.

As for memorable tries I've scored at Knowsley Road, I remember playing against Sheffield a few years ago and I was just coming back from a hernia operation. I remember going down the left flank to score. It was just nice to get back and score that try. I'll never forget Mr Scott, who is the hernia surgeon at Fairfield Hospital, I went to see him to get the all clear in the morning. He watched the game and when I went to see him again he said: "When I told you to go easy on that hernia I meant it" after seeing me running down the pitch.

You've got to say the Bradford last minute try [in the 2000 play offs] stands out. It doesn't bother me who scores, as long as Saints win that's all I'm bothered about. Regarding that try, you're always in with a chance of winning the game as long as there's time on the clock. There was time on the clock that night, be it only seconds. I was anticipating the kick and if you watch it on video I was probably stood 30 yards in front of the ball. Being a player you're always coached to keep behind the ball. The next thing that happened was Westy's flicked a few opponents off down the wing and I was on his inside to support and score what was a magnificent try and something that people will talk about for years and years to come.

Once you win things and you get in the habit of winning things, you want more. That's the case with myself. We've been to the last two Grand Finals, we've won three Challenge Cups and really I just don't like losing. You want to win everything and that becomes a good habit. If you've had success you want more. It's like anything, if you're used to 100 quid a week, you want it every week. That's exactly the same regarding my career. I have a number of goals I'd like to achieve in the game. I've never won the Lance Todd trophy, that would be something I'd like to achieve.

My contract runs out this year so it's a big year for me because I've got to prove to the club that I'm worthy of another contract. It will inspire me to play well this season. I can back my own ability and we'll see what happens come the end of the year.

I want to stay at the club: two of the factors in that are moving to a new stadium and also my testimonial year. They will be big incentives for me. I know everybody at Saints and because we're effectively moving into a bigger organisation there's going to be new people to meet and that gives you your hunger. Andy Farrell is a good friend of mine and was at Wigan for some years playing at Central Park for eight years. He said when they moved to the JJB stadium: "You know what, it's like being at a new club". Those words will spur me on if I do sign again.

I will sadly miss Knowsley Road but life will go on. If I can have half the memories in the new stadium as I have had at Knowsley Road I will not be going too far wrong and maybe, just maybe, I'll get a hot shower after the game.

Ian Millward

Ian made his name as part of the coaching staff of Illawarra Steelers in Australia after a neck injury had cut short his playing career. He moved to England to take the Leigh coaching job in the Northern Ford Premiership. He turned a struggling side into a top of the table outfit. When Ellery Hanley was sacked from Knowsley Road in the spring of 2000 Ian took over the coaching role, a position he holds to this day, with his first game in charge being Hull FC away on the 17

March, a game that Saints won. In a little over 12 months, Ian has coached Saints to Grand Final success over Wigan at Old Trafford. Then a first ever Saints World Club Championship after the team's superb victory over Brisbane Broncos and to complete the treble, clean sweep of trophies Saints went on to defeat Bradford Bulls at Twickenham in April 2001 to lift the Challenge Cup. Ian will go down in the history books as one of the most successful Saints coaches ever.

I had some preconceived impressions of the ground because I knew it was a famous club, I knew it was a famous ground. I had some preconceived ideas from when Australia had played St Helens here and Kangaroo tours were pretty special in Australia. So in the back of my mind I knew it had all this history and nostalgia about it. The biggest thing I found was that it was a bit of a buzz for me to go down to the old dressing rooms where people like Tommy Bishop and Cliff Watson who had played in Australia and who I had met and knew had been and of course people like Alex Murphy. It was a privilege to be in the same dressing room that they had used. It struck me first as a bit of an older ground, it's got that sort of mystique about it and you think "'wow" and you get there and it's a Rugby League ground. I think it's just all the great players here and the teams that make it just feel like something special.

When first approached to take the Saints job, I was a bit apprehensive to be honest. You know I didn't rush into it. There was a couple of reasons. There was some unsettled people at the club, if you look off the field there was some internal problems. History shows that a team in major leagues that wins a comp does tend to struggle the next year. I'm not talking about when Wigan won it year after year, but in a competitive league, which Super League is. Players get demotivated, they lose sight of the things they do, they get distracted by outside things. Timing is all important in coaching because you only get so many opportunities. If you get it wrong, you can't start at the bottom and work your way back up. You actually fall off the shelf. That's where I'm really proud of the players. They kicked on and went to another level in 2000 and have moved onto another level in 2001.

What made my mind up to take the job was not the players because I didn't know them. The thing that made me want to go to Saints was in the big global game they're a big name, there's a lot of history behind them, they're a great club, it's a Rugby League town and I just thought with all that, it had all the ingredients of a good culture and a great desire.

I don't want to get negative on any technical things, every coach has his own thoughts, there was some technical things I was looking forward to getting my hands on after being with them at training for a while. They had a really good work ethic. They were prepared to train hard which was good too. Over a period of time, I found they were a bunch of guys that had a great desire to be successful. They wanted to be continually challenged, they wanted new ideas all the time. They were prepared to change their ways if that had to happen for them to continue to be successful. Attacking wise, we changed the way we played. We changed the way people actually caught the ball, we asked them to stand in different positions. We asked people to take on different roles defensively. We asked some people to take a look at their defensive technique. We just wanted to keep abreast of our opposition and keep abreast of the times.

The modern game dictates that players must be multi skilled, it's another thing when you don't have a big squad to have to become multi skilled. As a player, I don't think it's a good thing to be pigeonholed. You get enjoyment from learning new roles, for some players it also opens up their representative career. That's my philosophy and it's something that we do practice in training. It comes with your skill work. Your skill work identifies how you handle different situations in a game so regardless what your position you play whether you are a front rower or a centre your skill work enables you to react to that situation.

On my first day at Saints, it is a true story that I ended up being locked in my office. I got to the ground early in the morning, was discussing a contract with the club, that was drawn out for a while then we had a press conference at 1pm. I couldn't get over how many people were here, that hit home to me how big a club Saints were. After that I addressed the players, then I did some more meeting of staff, addressed the Alliance people, then got to my office, locked myself in and started doing a lot of video work for the Hull game that was upcoming. Nobody expected anyone to be in my office late so they all left and locked me in.

My first game in charge at Knowsley Road was the game against Wakefield which we won. The main thing I remember about that is the try that Tommy scored when Sean had gone to kick a penalty, missed and Tommy caught it to dive over. I'll tell you what I did. I didn't really know Eric Ashton. I was sitting near the directors in the stand. Sean's took the shot at goal, Tommy's come through and scored, I turned to Eric Ashton and shouted "Hey". He looked up and said "What" as if to say what's the coach singing about? I said "We practised that during the week". At first he smiled and then he realised I was taking the mick out of him. He responded in kind and I just started laughing. It was sort of weird. It was a pretty close game that, at no time did I think we were probably going to lose. I've been really lucky over the last three or four years, even before I came over from Australia where I was reserve grade coach and assistant coach. Over there the reserve grade team finished second and we got knocked out in the semis, the year before that the team I had finished second and got knocked out, with Leigh we were winning the majority of our games so you start to feel a little bit bullet proof.

You think very positive all the time. The atmosphere at that game was good, I think everyone appreciated what the players had done the week before at Hull because mentally it was very tough on the players. It was tough on me mentally too.

The Saints' supporters are really good. Some games, they've probably been one of our best performers. It amazes me you know like at Old Trafford, Twickenham, sometimes at the JJB. I think the biggest one I remember from them was July 2000 when we were away at Wigan. We were down 16-0 early in the game and Iro went off early. We had gone into the game with a few injuries. The supporters just started chanting "We are the champions", because Wigan were just starting to get really bullish and their supporters were giving our supporters a bit. Our supporters also started singing "Oh when the Saints go marching in" which is a great song for the players, they really lift. Their supporters went dead quiet because even if you're winning 16-0 there's no comeback to "We are the champions". It just sort of give us a lift and we rode on the back of it. One thing the team does very well is that they respond, and the supporters got louder and the team got stronger and it ended up a great finish. I just think that in some really big games they've given us a huge lift and they've been great.

At times, the players and I are a little bit disappointed for what we've achieved, regardless of what day the side plays, or what's happened in the past or what people perceive of the Board, we just feel that the attendances should be a little bit higher. We feel we couldn't play any better, we couldn't give any more and our style of play is very entertaining and exciting. I don't know what the answer is because my answer is just to answer it on the pitch. What we've got to watch is that we don't get into a situation where we don't increase our crowds so we can't increase our ability to retain players or sign new ones. It looks all right at the moment but unless we continue to improve off the pitch we'll end up falling behind.

If someone had told me when I first took over at the club that the side would take out all three trophies available I wouldn't have believed them. When I got the job, my main thoughts were with the conflict outside and inside the club, with the player's attitudes at that time. I'll be honest with you, to me it looked like there was about three sections within the players at that time. There were some that were anti, some that didn't care less and some were for. I felt that there was about three distinct sections. I didn't go into it too much. My main thoughts when I took the job were to make the play offs. I thought if we did that it's shown that we've won more than we've lost. It shows we're moving in the right direction and it gives us a chance to mount a defence. At no time, did we talk any different. What I did say to the players was that our goal, which sounds a simple one, was just to make the play offs. If with five or six games to go we've a chance of achieving something else we'll re-evaluate it and we did. With about six games to go I said: "Look, I think we're a good chance of finishing top of the league". That was our new goal, we just kept that private. Come the last league game, if we had won we would have finished top of the league.

At Old Trafford when we won the Grand Final I only made it back to the dressing room very late. By the time I had spoken to all the media and everything, I was quite late back. I always seem to be the last one off the pitch. I take a slow walk and I walk with my kids. I usually team up with Tommy or I grab Wello, you know someone who really loves the place. Some of them, I think, walk too quick! I like to enjoy it. At Old Trafford by the time I had done the press conference and got to our dressing room they had all showered.

The World Club Challenge was great, I made sure I got back to the dressing room and it was awesome. With the World Club Challenge, I couldn't get over how satisfied the English players were with beating Brisbane and couldn't believe they were the best team in the world. Players like Newlove were very excited. That to me was really special. Twickenham, I just made a point with the media "hands off". I did the lap and then went straight to the dressing room. There was people outside the door waiting for me to go to the BBC. I just told them to go away. After a while, we had the champagne, it was a really good atmosphere in there, we were getting our photo taken. It was great, I just said to Longy: "Are you ready to go mate?" He said "Yeah". Everyone was having a shower and he said: "Let's get going now" so me and him went up to the BBC studio then. You learn from the first one. They're all good. The first one takes a while to sink in, the second one you knew you had climbed a really high mountain, the third one I was just really chilled out to be honest.

The biggest pressure game I've ever had since coming to this club was Leeds in the semi final. There was a lot of pressure on me there. Over half of the players hadn't been to a Challenge Cup final so the majority of the squad hadn't won a Challenge Cup medal. There was no pressure on me from the Board but I could see they were desperate to go money wise. The other one was the fans, the club hadn't been to the final since 1997 so it had been a bit of a wait. They were desperate to get there. So there was pressure from players, the Board and the fans, people kept saying: "Just get us to that

Challenge Cup final, Ian". You have to remember it constitutes a holiday for some of the fans who go away for a couple of days to watch the game.

Some people may have thought my big pressure game would have been the Grand Final against Wigan but the pressure isn't on me as much against Wigan now. As much as I am heavily involved with the rivalry and I believe in it and all that is that I've got a good record against Wigan. Not like some previous coaches where if they get beat it becomes the better of them. It doesn't worry me that.

We started talking about the World Club Challenge as soon as we won at Old Trafford. I was really excited about it. When we got back into training, we spoke about it. Then we went away to Lanzarote for a week and spoke about the game over there. What we showed the players very early in the preparation was a lot of tapes showing where we thought Brisbane were vulnerable. That gave the players confidence. I just told the players that I thought we deserved a shot at the World Club Championship and that we were a World Championship team. I basically said to the players that if we got beaten I would be very disappointed. I said if you play the way I know you can and you play to the game plan I've asked you to then we won't get beaten. I really believed that and the others believed it too. You can tell they believed it because when we were behind we didn't panic. We just stuck to it and stuck to it and eventually come home.

I said to the players at half time and this sounds really weird and I've never done it since but I believed it because the first 20 minutes of the second half is the Broncos' best time of the game. They throw their best 20 minutes at you then. We were down 12-6 at half time. I said to them: "Look, I'm going to give you bad news here but there's a silver lining. I think they'll score first. There's a good chance they'll blow the score out to 18-6 but if you can hold them to one try, I think you'll find that we'll be too strong for them in the last 20 minutes. I think we've got the right tactics, the right key people and we've got some great players and if you can keep them to one try you're well on the way to victory". So when Brisbane scored, I think it was good for the players because usually if you concede a try

108

straight after half time you're really down about it but instead it was like: "Well we knew this was going to happen so we can just live with it" and it was alright.

People ask me which trophy has given me the most personal pleasure. The Challenge Cup was great because it's got so much tradition in the world of Rugby League. Some great players and coaches from Australia have won it. I thought it was special to be a part of history especially with it being the hundredth Challenge Cup. The Grand Final was my first Premiership win. That was great and made me feel good because until you win one that monkey's always on your back. We'd been flogged in the last league game against Wigan then we played sensational against Bradford, sensational against Wigan and sensational in the Grand Final. We peaked at the right time, we learnt from mistakes. We did everything right. The Brisbane win gives you real satisfaction. We were long odds on not to win. We were playing the best team in the world and this and that. That was a really great win. It's really hard for me to pick, one day I'll say one then the next day I'll pick one of the others. They're all great. One thing we have learnt from the three is that we have learned how to handle big games. We know how to prepare the players, how to get them ready. There's a real knack to it I feel and I think we've got it down pat.

Winning the three trophies makes me feel great. You put the hard work in and it's the icing on the cake. You still put the hard work in whether you win or lose. It's a famous club, it's going to be here for another 100 years and just to be part of history and to go down with some of the great players and coaches, it's awesome. I remember I said after we won the Challenge Cup we might not be the greatest side of all time but when people talk about the great teams we'll be there. That's good. People don't realise just how hard we do work, I've always said this to the players with regards contracts, "Recognition is a by-product of success". If you're doing well whether you're a player or a coach then recognition comes with that. If we get put up there with the rest then that's a privilege.

It's incredible with what we've done considering that on the money scale we're probably about fourth on the list. It's an unbelievable achievement.

Every player is different and everyone has a different make up. They've each got a different temperament and different skills. It's very hard with a squad of 25 to talk to everyone individually a lot. The thing is, to be honest with them. We're a very calm dressing room on game day, before the game, at half time and after the game. We work hard during the week. Just from an individual's point of view we try and give as much feedback as we can. We try and be positive, we don't use the negative word too much. What we use is areas where we think we can improve you. Everyone says to me: "How did you find going to St Helens? It must have been a big difference for you". That's what I'm used to though. I started coaching at Illawarra Steelers in 1993 and I left at the end of 1998. I worked my way up to reserve grade coach and assistant first grade coach. I dealt with Paul McGregor, Rod Wishart, Brad Mackay and Trent Barrett. All of whom were really good players. I was full-time so that was the environment I was used to. It wasn't a culture change for me when I came to St Helens. I had a foundation, I've never done everything right and I've made mistakes along the way but I've had time to assess them, look at doing things differently and updating ideas and that's one of the big crux's in coaching is having a foundation.

The second thing is I think one of my strengths is man management. I find it comfortable talking with the players and being honest with them. I remember one game at Knowsley Road that we had won pretty easily. I came into the dressing room and I was yahooing and Chris Joynt said: "Bloody hell, you're a bit excited today". I just said: "Yeah, what a great win, you played awesome". He pulled me to one side later and said: "You know what, you've taught me in regard to that I'm a person who doesn't show my emotion a lot, you show it". I said: "You've got to because we've worked bloody hard and we've done everything right, show it".

I think emotionally the players are strong. Chris is a great leader. I'm always encouraging Sean and Keiron, especially before big games, to come out and be laughing and having a bit of yahooing. It takes the stress out.

Sports science is unbelievable and it's going to continue that way. However, unless you can do it you're always going to fall behind and that's the art of coaching. There's some people out there who can come up with great ideas but they can't deliver it. You can take a horse to water but you can't make it drink. I can come up with all the ideas but if the players don't go out and do it or don't believe in it then it's useless. You'd like to spend more and more time with the players but as long as you get the technical things right that's the important thing. Sports science is very important but the art of the game is just as important and being able to deliver it is just as important.

Having my son Robbie with me at games keeps me keep in check with reality. He never talks unless he's asked to. He's just very regimented now, he just sort of hangs there. I'll never forget playing Wigan in the play-offs last year and I was sat there and I said to him just after half time: "How do you think we're going?" and he said: "I think we're playing real good Dad" and I said: "I do too mate". Then with about 15 minutes to go I said: "What do you reckon mate?" and he said: "I think we're going to Old Trafford, Dad". He's smart because he's been around football. He's not a kid who would ask: "Can I go and do this?" or whatever. He never affects what I'm doing. When I talk to the players, he gets right out of the road. It makes me feel good to have him there. If things are going bad it's a reminder that you've got a family. It makes you realise that I can enjoy it with him and leave him with good memories.

As for my most special moment at Knowsley Road so far, well you've probably got to look at some of the Wigan games haven't you? They're the special ones. My first Wigan game here, we gave them a touch up. We were pretty hot that day. Beating Wigan in the Challenge Cup at the ground. People don't realise but they talk about the big four in Rugby League. We had to beat the other three of the big four to win the Challenge Cup, Bradford only had to beat one of them. Naturally the Bradford game here in 2000 with the last second Chris Joynt try. We'd come off a big loss against Wigan the week before and there was reasons why we'd lost. I'll never forget this, with about two minutes to go in the Bradford game I turned to my assistant and said: "You know what, I'm proud of these blokes. We've played awesome, I can't believe we're going to lose. We don't deserve to lose. The effort we've put in and the way they've turned things around we just don't deserve to lose". They kicked down field and then bang, bang we scored. I thought: "I can't believe that". So the Wigan games and that Bradford one have been the special ones and I think there's more to come. There's the Australian game and I'd like to win that. It all goes on how healthy everyone is.

Keeping the success going is dependent on a number of factors. It's about getting the chemistry right with the players. I think we've got the right chemistry with youth and experience. The support of the fans on the terraces, that's vital. Sponsorship is another one. We have to all keep challenging ourselves, coaches and players, to keep one step ahead of the opposition and keep trying to better ourselves.

As for my ambitions within the game, I'd like to keep winning trophies at St Helens. When I think the time is right, I'd like to go back and coach in the NRL. I have had a couple of opportunities to go back already but I'm working with a real good bunch of players here. They've got a great desire, I love working with them. The grass isn't always greener on the other side of the fence. Why leave something that's great? It's all about timing.

I think that the new stadium is going to be exciting. It will be great for the team and the club, I think you'll find that a lot of people will be really refreshed like they're at a new club. Hopefully, I can keep bettering myself. I'd hate to think what I'm doing now I'm doing in a couple of years time. I'd like to progress myself. I've been lucky since I've been at the club that it's been all good times. Good times with the players, I enjoy the smile on their faces, I try and keep my body language in check too. It's just enjoyable working with them and I just hope we can continue.

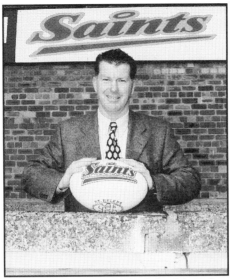
Ian Millward on the day he joined St Helens
(Photo: Bernard Platt)

I will be coaching Saints in the last game at Knowsley Road unless
they get rid of me! It will be special and what makes it more special
is what we've achieved. Like if we hadn't have won anything, you'd
be looked at as just: "Oh, he coached there for a few seasons" but it's
a special time, it's a special team. I think it's a great way to finish the
ground off with a special team. That means a lot. I think going down
in history as the last coach at Knowsley Road, they say you're only
as good as your last game and we'll be involved in it. I think it's
awesome. It's been a selling point with some players I've spoken to
about coming here.

Andrew Quirke with the three trophies won by Ian Millward's St Helens
team - Super League Trophy, the Challenge Cup and the World Club
Challenge Trophy (Photo: courtesy Andrew Quirke)

Players' entrance   One of the turnstiles

(Photos: Top - Peter Lush, bottom - Chris Gill)

The main stand

Photos: Top: Peter Lush, middle: Andrew Quirke, bottom: Chris Gill

116

The dug-outs and the "Scaff" (Photo: Bernard Platt)

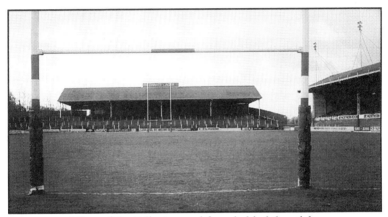

View of the Edington end from behind the sticks
at the restaurant end (Photo: Andrew Quirke)

Sky Sports big screen and the restaurant (Photo: Peter Lush)

Tunnels

Saints come out of the tunnel in the main stand (Photo: Peter Lush)

View from the "old" tunnel at the clubhouse end
(Photo: Andrew Quirke)

Saints Superstore (Photo: Peter Lush)

Saints 38 Wigan 14 - Good Friday 2000 (Photo: Kevin Gill)

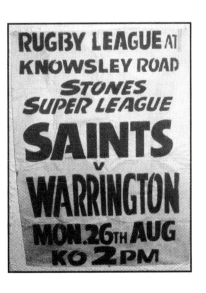

Poster for the St Helens versus Warrington match August 1996. The Saints' victory secured the Super League title for the club

(Photo: Andrew Quirke)

Some Saints heroes

Paul Newlove
(Photo: Bernard Platt)

Kevin Ward
(Photo: Bernard Platt)

Sean Long as St Bernard
(Photo: Bernard Platt)

Ellery Hanley
while coach at the
club (Photo:
Bernard Platt)

Programmes from memorable Knowsley Road matches

St Helens versus St Gaudions
(French champions)
5 June 1971.
Saints won 62-0.
(Permission from St Helens RFC)

Saints versus Castleford
7 October 1984.
Mal Meninga's debut for Saints.
St Helens won 30-16.
(Permission from St Helens RFC)

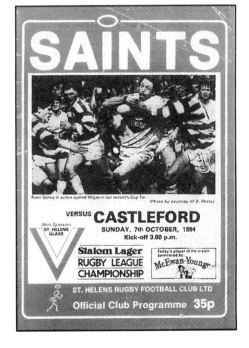

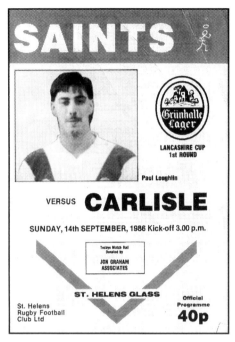

Saints versus Carlisle
14 September 1986 in the Lancashire Cup.
Saints won 112-0.

Saints against the Australian tourists
2 November 1986.
Saints lost 32-8.

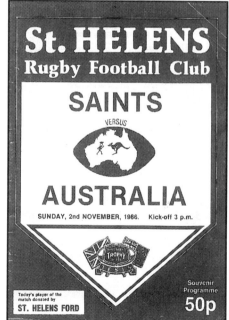

Part 2: Saints' Voices

Albert Barker
Jack Coatsworth
Gerry Moore
Ken Halsall
Tony Bennett
Mick Gill
Paul Bennett
Mike Critchley
Kevin
Linda Edwards
John Yates
Ste Rigby
James Michael
Chris
Mike
Andrew Quirke

Albert Barker

Albert, a long time supporter of the club and former vice-president of the club, has been watching Saints for more than 60 years. He still follows the team now.

One of the earliest games I remember going to was against Salford. The only reason I remember it was that they called them the "famous Red Devils". The players looked like giants to me at the time. Before the war, I remember Saints playing St Helens Recs, and I recall combined sides of Saints and Recs playing the touring sides. When the Kiwis played us they would always visit the house of Richard Seddon who was once their Prime Minister, he had lived on Prescot Road. When the Kiwis played us in the 1939-40 season they were then sent home after the match because of the onset of the war.

As a young boy, I remember there used to be queues outside the ground of people waiting to get in for free when they opened the gates for the last quarter of the game. There was very little money around in those days.

As a kid I also remember there being warning notices up at the ground about getting on to the referee. The crowd had a bit of a bad reputation for that. There were threats to shut the ground if there was any more bad behaviour from the crowd. I remember one Saints and Wigan match in 1944 that was abandoned due to crowd trouble.

The old wooden stand on the halfway line was the best spot on the ground, you used to get charged to get in there. They used to have fencing round the perimeter of the field like at Castleford today. Some supporters could bring chairs and sit inside the fencing, actually by the pitch. I suppose the club's view was that you could fit quite a few more people round the pitch. There were also trees, you used to get kids swinging in the trees watching the game. There was no terracing on the ground during the war years, it was all dirt and strips of wood. Under the old scoreboard, there used to be a sort of stall or shop that would sell programmes. After rationing, Bonney's sold sweets there. Bonney's were a local firm that had originated from the Gladstone Street area.

During the war, the ground was used as an ambulance station although they did try to carry on playing rugby for a while. They had road blocks at the ground, big concrete lumps that were nicknamed "tank traps". They were all over St Helens during the war, the idea was to roll them into the street in front of tanks. The trainers of the side in this era were the likes of Oliver Dolan, the ex Recs hooker, and Joe Carson.

Around this time, the pitch was also used to let Bates Gordon's cows graze. Around this time, local kids, including myself, would unload straw for the club and pack it at the back of the main stand and put straw over the touchline round the pitch.

I remember one match where Jimmy Myers wasn't at the ground. Someone said: "Myers hasn't arrived." I'm not surprised, he'd been captured at Dunkirk that weekend. We didn't see him for five years. No one knew where Myers was at that time including his family.

At the end of the war, a sort of novelty for supporters watching the A team play at home was listening to the tannoy at the end of the game for details of how the first team were getting on away. When Jimmy Stott came home from the war, it really was the big thing of the day. He played centre for Saints.

In those days and for a long time afterwards Boxing Day would always see Wigan come to Knowsley Road and we would always go to Central Park on Good Friday. When Jim Sullivan came to the club, he helped alter that so that the fixtures alternated. We were fourth off the bottom of the league before Sullivan came and turned things round for us.

In later years the wall was added to the ground. Then they built the terracing. The Edington stand came next, the speccies paid for it and Saints then charged them to go in it. George Edington had a paper shop on Knowsley Road and he was the main instigator of raising funds for the stand, that's why it was named after him.

I can tell you why the main stand doesn't go all the way along the length of the ground and instead stops at the 25-yard line. The club wanted to finish building it but the Rugby League wouldn't lend them the money they needed to complete the job. There were even plans to put Knowsley Road on stilts like Central Park at one point.

Speaking of things to do with Wigan, whenever we played them at Knowsley Road it was a match like no other. You would go through the turnstiles and the back of your neck would be tingling. They would shut the gates up to two hours before kick off. We played Wigan in the semi-final of the Lancashire Cup in 1947 and there was over 30,000 in the ground. It was packed.

A new scoreboard was introduced in the 1950s and was paid for by the Todd brothers. It was situated in the popular side corner of the ground at the clubhouse end.

When we played Australia in our centenary year the Aussie commentators couldn't get over Knowsley Road. They were saying what a fabulous ground it was. It's a ground where you feel you can reach out and touch the players. The playing surface is second to none.

For memorable games, I don't think you'll ever beat the Saints-Bradford match in 2000 when we won in the last second. The try that won us the game went through nine pairs of hands, it was incredible. It was a team try. The lad who made it, Dwayne West, did very well. He beat two men along the touchline and sent in Joynt. They took a chance and it came off.

The players

If we're talking about players I can remember, I've been watching Saints for around 65 years. I've probably seen players I can't remember. I started watching back in the early 1930s and I can certainly remember Alf Ellaby. But my boyhood hero was always Duggie Greenall so he stands out for me. He not only played for Saints but for his county and his country. He was the first local born international to represent Saints as a tourist for 20 years, other Saints players had played for England at home but never on tour.

Some of the players who starred for Saints before the war were the likes of Jack Fearnley, Peter Twist and Jack Waring who returned injured from the war after playing for England Rugby Union in Cairo. Among the players who kept Saints going during the war were Albert Butler the full-back, Mick Lawrence who could play

126

wing or centre, Tommy Waring, the youngest ever Saints player, who made his first team debut at just 15-and-a-half. The half-back pairing was Eddie Prescott at stand-off and Billy French at scrum-half, with a back row of Riley, Thompson and Mills.

I remember the Fishwick brothers, Ike the hooker and Bill the winger who later went on to play second-row. Ike went to Warrington when we signed Stan McCormick.

The best footballer I have ever seen in my life is Alex Murphy. If he played today he would be an absolute sensation. There used to be around 2,000 who used to watch Saints train at the time Duggie played. Peter Lyons, the trainer, used to be a sergeant major. He would line the players up in the middle of the pitch before training and do a roll-call to check they were all there. I remember a wonderful attacking stand-off we had by the name of Eric Hesketh. There was one occasion where he was running towards his own line and the crowd were laughing at him. All of a sudden, he stopped and swivelled round to score up the other end.

Saints signed many Welsh lads. There was Len Constance, Steve Llewellyn, Gullick, Lewis, Johnny Morris the scrum-half, the class centre Vivien Harrison, Ray Cale, George Parsons, the list went on and on. There was hundreds of them, all good players.

Len Aston was one of the great second-rowers of his era. Once, the ref blew up for a forward pass yet Len still had hold of the ball, he had just dummied and fooled everyone.

In the 1950s we had Peter Metcalfe, a good stand-off and Todder Dickinson another class half-back. Sadly, knee problems finished both their careers. There was also Frank McCabe, a very good hooker, who was the Keiron Cunningham of his day. Sadly, injury cut his career short too.

I remember van Vollenhoven's debut against Leeds in October 1957 when there was over 23,000 at Knowsley Road. His next game was also at Knowsley Road in the A team against Whitehaven where he scored two tries in front of more than 8,000 supporters.

The best Aussie we've had is Phil Veivers. He was a good servant to the club and a good player. I've always said that one man doesn't make a team, but there was one player who came here though, and only played a handful of games, yet had a massive impact on the team and that was Mal Meninga in 1984-85.

Memories

We were playing Bradford here in a cup tie one year and Peter Lyons took the team to Billinge Hill. Bradford were already at the ground in the home team dressing room while Lyons was encouraging his players to breathe in the fresh air on top of the "lump". There wasn't long to kick off and traffic was building up along the East Lancs. Saints arrived just 40 minutes before the kick off.

Lionel Swift, who was on the board, would sometimes go into the dressing room at half time to offer the players 10 bob [50p] extra if they won. Ernie Mills, the groundsman, once found a shoulder-pad type protective device after a match against Bradford. Back in those days, wearing such protection was illegal but the game had been played and they got away with it. So, all those who think that shoulder pads are an invention of the modern game better think again as this was 1948! It never made the local press though.

I remember tales from my grandfather who would tell me about the old days where Lord Derby was president of Saints and gentlemen in the best stand would wear their top hats.

In 1956, there was a game where the pitch was frozen, so Saints put some big watchman's braziers on the pitch to heat it.

The funniest thing I've ever seen at the ground was a lady marching up and down the touchline bashing opposition players with her umbrella.

I'd say the finest Saints team I saw was 1952-53. The first time we went to Wembley we had a song that went: "We ain't got a barrel of money, we've got Langfield and Honey, with Duggie and Llew, running 'em through, side-by-side".

I think my worst memory at Knowsley Road is the year Wigan were relegated and we played Oldham for our traditional festive fixture in the 1980-81 season. There was no atmosphere at all. I'm not a Wiganer, I'm a Saints fan through and through but I'm a Rugby League supporter. Saints and Wigan need each other for the gates, the rivalry and the atmosphere. If they went, what other game would mean the same?

I'm for progress. After going to the JJB Stadium and such, that's what I want Saints' ground to be like.

Another thing that should be mentioned about the ground is that in the past you would never see many women at Knowsley Road. That has changed now, if it wasn't for women coming to Saints we would really struggle for crowds. It's about women and kids now, families. So, an all-seater stadium makes it more attractive for them. You've got to cater for people.

Jack Coatsworth

Jack Coatsworth has been a Saints supporter for 64 years. For more than a decade, he worked as a dressing-room assistant at the club and shared in many of the Saints teams' most memorable moments including walking across the hallowed turf of Wembley. Jack finished working in the dressing room in the late 1990s.

I can't really remember much about the first game that I saw at Knowsley Road because I was only about five years old. This would be around 1935. I remember going up to the ground with my father and him lifting me over the turnstiles. He took me in between the 25-yard line and the halfway line of the popular side and sat me on the wooden fencing around the ground. This wooden fencing was painted with lime whitewash. After a game sitting on the fence and being a young lad wriggling about, I would have to be dusted down to remove the lime.

As I got a little older, probably about eight years of age, I decided I would go with one of my friends. We would walk to the ground from Haresfinch, along Washaway Lane, through Windle City past the old Recs ground. I remember Recs and the ding-dong struggles they had with Saints. I didn't have many years experience of that though, because they folded when I was young. There was always a good crowd on when Saints played Recs. I do remember the atmosphere in town when Saints were about to play Recs. Men would argue about it, it was like a religion. You were either Recs or Saints. I do remember men putting the red, amber and black flag out when Recs had won like people do for royal visits. It was intense because you were living with them. You get the same sort of bitterness today whenever Saints play Wigan. I was always a Saints supporter as a boy because my father had played for them and later supported them. He was a Saints die-hard and I grew up in that same frame of mind.

Anyway, when we'd walked past Recs, we would go along Bishop Road then up Rivington Road to the ground. In those days, it was amazing, the crowd would come from all directions. All roads led to Knowsley Road as it were. There weren't cars and it was unbelievable the amount of people walking to the ground, you can't picture it. There were buses from town that used to run from Shaw Street. As you got to Knowsley Road they were coming in droves from all directions. The streets were packed solid with people walking along talking rugby. In those days it was common to get 15,000 for an ordinary match. When we started to really play well under Jim Sullivan we would get 30,000 or more for the bigger games like Wigan.

Taylor Park was full of a wave of people coming from Thatto Heath, a real Rugby League area where a lot of players came from.

I remember going down to the ground with many others at 8a.m. on matchday to clear straw from the pitch. We would get a free ticket for the match for doing this. It was like gold, getting a free ticket for Saints. Money was so scarce in those days even though it was very cheap to watch Saints back then. I used to stand in the boys' pen which had railings round it to keep us all in. You could get out when your father came to collect you. The ground had railway sleepers as steps at this time.

Games were played in atrocious conditions in those days yet the matches still went on. I remember a game played against Italy at the end of one season. They had cleared all the grass off the pitch to resurface it in time for the next season in the late forties and the players played on a pitch with no grass. Joe Pickavance, the director, worked with Eric Edwards to make sure they got a good drainage system. They got a machine that made holes in the pitch during the close season. They put a mixture of sand, seed and peat into those holes and the pitch matured. Neil Holding did the same in later years as does John Edwards today.

At the top end of the clubhouse on a little stand was a simple scoreboard. It had T, G, DG and PTS along the top with St Helens and Visitors going along the side. The person operating it would just slip numbers onto the board.

Walking around the ground would be a lad with a board on a huge pole, with the team changes for the day. All the pubs and shops in town would display a team sheet on a Thursday before the match on a Saturday. Most matches would be played at 3p.m. on a Saturday.

There was a wooden stand on the popular side stretching from the 25 yard line of the Dunriding Lane end to the try line of the Kop end. That stand, when we got rid of it, was given to Liverpool City.

The Kop in those days was just a banking of cinders and railway sleepers. Behind the stand, on the best side, ran a railway line. This came from Triplex, it ran along the back of Saints, to a factory in the centre of St Helens.

St Helens, as a ground, has changed so much over the years. A lot of credit has to go to the various boards of directors who have spent considerable money on the venue over time.

The Yearsley bothers, who were on the board, had a building firm. They decided that the ground needed building up. They introduced terracing and concrete steps. They improved the ground considerably. The Edington stand and best side stand were added while the Yearsley brothers were there. So, all the ground had terracing. The wall around the ground was also added. The dugout, in those days, was directly opposite where it is today. It used to be on the best side. It used to go into a dip like the policeman's dugouts at each corner of the ground.

When you've seen something come from a very dilapidated type of ground to a good ground by Rugby League standards, then there is sadness to leave it behind. Having said that, you've got to progress. I'm all for moving, but it is tinged with a little sadness over leaving behind the ground.

131

Players

As for great players, I remember the latter days of Alf Ellaby. He was the star wingman of the time. He had gone to Wigan and just come back to Saints when I saw him, the very end of his career. I remember my father saying to me: "There'll never be another Ellaby". Of course, I was lucky enough to see another who was an immortal wingman in the shape of Tom van Vollenhoven. He was brilliant, he had everything. Ellaby was a very good wingman who could score tries. Vollenhoven though could score tries, tackle, read a game and so on. The try he scored at Odsal in the Championship Final of 1959 against Hunslet was unforgettable, even the Hunslet players were shaking their heads. Then of course there was the try he scored at Wembley in 1961, particularly because it was against Wigan, but they were just a couple of many that you could pick out.

I remember Duggie Greenall colliding with one of the posts once and the top snapped off and it just missed hitting him. If it had hit him it would have killed him, no question about it. He just got up, shrugged it off and carried on playing. That was the sort of player Duggie Greenall was. When he tackled players, they lay down.

Then you have the likes of Mal Meninga, some of the tries he scored for Saints were amazing. Billy Benyon was the coach in those days and I had just started helping out in the dressing room at the time. I stayed there until Ellery Hanley came. Unfortunately my back went at that time. I finished assisting in the dressing room then, but I had some smashing years there.

There's so many good tries and games from 1936 right up to the present day that it is impossible to go through them all. Look at the Chris Joynt try in 2000 in the play-off match against Bradford, who could forget that? That try will be remembered by the younger element of supporters for years and years to come.

Going back to the early years though, we were always signing Welsh players at the club. We signed players like Glanville Jones, Constance the stand-off and Lewis the second-row forward. When Jim Sullivan arrived at Saints, he decided to add a full-back to his then strong squad of players. Glyn Moses had travelled north to join his elder brother at Salford. He obviously didn't enjoy it at the Willows and returned back to Wales. Sully recognised his potential and, after contacting him, he returned to join the Saints. He was soon made to feel at home, joining the contingent of other Welsh players in the squad: Steve Llewellyn, Don Gullick, George Parsons and Ray Cale. He became one of the best full-backs to play for St Helens and must have enjoyed it. I say this because he eventually settled in the town to live here as did Steve Llewellyn and Roy Mathias. John Mantle later followed him, of course it would be remiss of me not to mention Kel Coslett who was a good clubman and superb goal kicker. Then, of course, in later years came Scott Gibbs. At the moment, we have two who play in the A team, Gareth Price and another lad called Howells. I don't know whether they will make the first team.

I've been very fortunate because when I first started watching Saints the forwards were called the "easy six". The team was known as the "handrags". You would hear people say: "Are you going to watch the handrags today?" This was because the team was so poor. Peter Lyons became coach and he started talking rugby to them. He was into his fitness and he had his players as fit as fiddles. We had players who wanted to play such as Vinty Karalius, he was a fitness fanatic. We had a lot of good players but Peter Lyons didn't seem to blend them properly.

They decided to part with Lyons and the new coach was Jim Sullivan. He came in the early 1950s and straight away he transformed Alan Prescott into a world beater. Then you had Alex Murphy, the best scrum-half that's ever lived in my eyes. Sullivan moulded the team together, you had a good scrum-half and a good loose-forward, there was Jim Honey at stand-off who could run, Dick Huddart a strong running second-row alongside Brian Briggs who would tackle and tackle for you. I've sat with coaches at Saints and they'll say: "Just watch so-and-so tackling", because they've said that you notice how much work some players get through yet they get no recognition.

You had Vinty at the back of the scrum though. If anyone from the opposition came round the blind side, Vinty would have them and they would go down. He was as hard as nails, he came over from the Isle of Man recently when Eric Hughes was coach and I showed him the player's gym. His eyes opened wide, he said: "If I'd have had this when I played". When he played for Saints, he actually built his own gym at home in an outhouse. He was the first person to bring that side of training into the game. He was a real character as well.

From when Jim Sullivan took over in the early 1950s we've always been a top team. I've had wonderful years following the Saints. That's what makes you happy.

In the dressing room

Working in the dressing room, you blend in with the players. You become part of the comradeship. If anybody ever tells you that there is ill-feeling within the dressing room, don't believe it. I worked for something like 18 years in that dressing room and I never saw an argument in there once. It reminded me of my time doing national service in the forces, you never had an argument there and it's the same at Saints.

I've been lucky because I was doing something that I loved. I grew up talking about rugby, rugby, rugby. It was a privilege to be able to help in the dressing room.

Before a big game, the backroom staff must learn to keep a distance. The players are naturally hyped up. You shouldn't in any way start pestering them or mithering them over petty little things. If they want you they will shout for you. The ideal thing is to relax and let the players relax. You shouldn't show any excitement. We make sure their kit is ready and serve them with anything they might need.

Some players like to talk to each other before a game. Others like to sit and relax and keep calm. They tend to focus their minds on the game. The players then join the circle where they encourage each other to get built up for the game. Nobody would upset any of the players before the game. The atmosphere in there is electric. At the same time though, they are well prepared. They have plenty of drinks to stop them getting dehydrated.

Jack Coatsworth at Wembley after the 1996 Challenge Cup final victory
(Photo: Bernard Platt)

Super League Champions - Saints The Entertainers
(Photo: Peter Lush)

Certain players were always very calm. The one I'll always remember is Shane Cooper, he was very quiet. He didn't want to be disturbed, he would just sit there and focus himself in readiness for the game. I think he showed that on the field because Shane was a good player and a very good reader of the game.

All players have their own little whims and beliefs. Some like to go out last, some want to go out straight after the captain, they all have little superstitions. They tend to do the same things in the same way before every match.

They're a great bunch of lads, I never had a problem with any of them. They're wonderful and have been throughout all my years there with them in the dressing room.

I remember sitting on the bench at Wembley in 1996 when Bradford were beating us 26-12. I was sat with the Saints doctor and we thought it might be all over for Saints. Vila Matautia was sat next to me and said: "We've not lost yet, there's 80 minutes in this game." Him saying that stuck in my mind. Of course, we won.

Every coach I worked with was different, they all had their own beliefs and approach. Every one of them I worked with have been masters of their trade. Even coaches that never won cups such as Eric Hughes were wonderful in their own way. The coaches appreciate everyone in the dressing room who works there and helps, the physios, the masseurs, the kitman Stan Wall and myself. All the coaches I worked with were smashing. I didn't spend time working with Ellery Hanley as my back went but all the players stated that he was a strict disciplinarian.

The people in the background like myself know the condition of Knowsley Road. If you go to the new stadium at Wigan, it is fabulous. I've been behind the scenes at their new stadium to have a look around and it is top class. Look at Widnes' ground, that is superb. I'm looking forward to seeing our new ground. I'm certain I'll be shown round it because when I go to games now they still invite me into the dressing room and so on. I will miss Knowsley Road though, you're bound to when you've been there for so many years. When I go past it and see houses built on it, that will be strange.

136

The memories are the main thing I'll have from Knowsley Road. All the matches that I've seen there and so on. The big crowds that were there. Playing Wigan there in front of 30 odd thousand. They locked the gates one year against Wigan and they broke the gates down by where the old wooden scoreboard used to be. People just didn't want to miss the match, they were sat on top of the Edington stand watching. I'll miss the old dressing rooms and the new dressing rooms, which were a big improvement. I worked in both. I will miss Knowsley Road but I'm looking forward to the new stadium.

Gerry Moore

Gerry has watched Saints for more than 60 years. As well as seeing numerous players and coaches come and go he spent 27 years working the old wooden scoreboard at the ground. He is also chairman of the supporters' club.

The outbreak of war, in 1939, is when I first started watching Saints. I stood against the whitewash fence on the popular side and it was just a fence, there was no wall around the pitch in those days. Me and the lad I went with didn't have a clue what was going on during the game. We had moved from town to Dunriding Lane and when I saw all the men walking past the house on a matchday. I asked my mum where they were all going. My mum told me they were going to Saints and it wouldn't happen now but at seven years of age I asked: "What's Saints?" Of course, my dad was a St Helens Recs supporter and said: "Don't mention that team in this house". My mum made him give me threepence to go to the game. That was the start, I've been here ever since. I used to stand in the boys' pen, its turnstile is where the supporters' club office is now. The railings to the boys' pen are still there, why they've never taken them down I don't know. It was a tanner to go in the Pen. When I got older I was allowed to go on the terracing which cost nine pence. A gang of us used to go to the top end including a friend of mine called Bernie Clifton.

All I ever heard people talking about in those days was Jimmy Stott. I remember thinking when he gets out of the army no one is going to touch Saints. When he came back, they used to have a van going round town with a megaphone saying: "Saints are at home today and Jimmy Stott is playing," to try and get people to go to the game.

I've been a supporters' club member since I was a kid. My involvement with the committee started in 1960 when I filled in as a bingo caller at Saints. At the interval during the bingo Len Kilshaw, Jack Gill and George Cotton approached me and asked if I wanted to be co-opted onto the committee and that was it, I was on.

Multi-purpose ground

Over the years, I've seen various sports at the ground. We had the Harlem Globetrotters basketball team. They put a big wooden board down in the middle of the field. Just after the war years, in front of the main stand as it was then they had a boxing exhibition with Peter Kane from Golborne who had been world champ and Brian London's dad old Jack London putting on matches.

On two occasions they've had Walls funfair out on the training pitch. At least twice they also had a circus out there as well, I remember this because I used to feed buns to the elephants.

They also had a home guard display at the ground. Where the kop is now they used to have a shale banking, there was a battered old car on there. Someone appeared at the end of the players' entrance with a bazooka, they only blew the car up didn't they.

I remember one time we had a team here called the Shape Indians, they were the Supreme Allied Headquarters Europe team, made up of Italians, Americans and so on. Saints played them at Knowsley Road. I can tell you the day, Monday 7 May 1962. The reason I remember it is that it was the day my daughter Angela was born, you can't forget that can you?

I remember standing in the boys' pen watching Saints play Carcassonne one year trying to get my programme autographed. I'll never forget it, the French team had a rubber stamp with all their signatures on that they would put on your programme. It's the first time I'd ever seen anything like it and I've not seen it since.

The supporters club shop. (Photo: Chris Gill)

As for where I've stood at Knowsley Road, well for 20-odd years I stood in the scoreboard, operating it. Now I sit in an end seat in the stand, I have to get an end seat because occasionally I have to move a sponsor's car. Before a game, I take it in turns to open the sponsor's car park which has to be open three hours before the game. I also organise coaches for away games. My main job is an hour before the kick-off when I meet the young mascots for the day. I give them a tour of the gym and other facilities before they lead the team out. I did it for one match temporarily about three years ago and I'm still doing it now.

I remember one guy, a Saints fanatic, Dick Hughes, God rest his soul. He always wore a flat cap and everytime you mentioned van Vollenhoven's name Dick would doff his cap. I remember talking to him years ago before the season started telling him that a hole had appeared on the ground, it was six or seven feet across, it must be an old well or something that had given way. It was about 10 in the morning that I told him this. When I went for my dinner someone else came to me and said: "What about this hole at Saints? It's about 30 feet across". I realised then how rumours start. Of course, the hole was eventually repaired and filled in.

Players

I don't like picking players out, there have been so many good Saints players over the years that I'm bound to miss some out so I can't pick a best ever 13 or whatever. The game has changed so much over the years, unlimited tackles, four tackles, six tackles and so on. However, the one who stands out above all others is Tommy Voll. He made the biggest impression. I remember when he was over here when Papua New Guinea played New Zealand at Knowsley Road in the World Cup in 1995. Tommy agreed to do the half-time draw on the pitch. I remember going up for Tommy at half-time to do the draw and I said to the steward on A stand that I was looking for Tommy Voll. The steward laughed and said: "He is not in here, I should know, I used to hero worship the bloke". Of course Tommy was wearing glasses and you always think of him how he looked when he played, you don't think of him ageing in any way. So Tommy shouted: "I'm here Gerry", the steward was gobsmacked and got Voll's autograph.

I took Tommy to the tunnel where he did the draw and was announced to the crowd. I was supposed to take him back to his seat in the stand. Of course, all the Popular side were shouting and whatever. So Voll says: "Come on let's go for a walk around the pitch." We walked all the way round the pitch and as we got to the corner at the scoreboard end he said: "My first try was here." He went on: "It's amazing this, there's little kids chasing me for my autograph and I bet their parents weren't even born when I played." I explained to him that he is folklore round here. He is a one and only that's for sure. He was the top one I have seen, way out in front, but then of course you can't forget Alex Murphy.

As for games at the ground that have generated the best atmosphere you've got to think about the cup tie against Wigan in 1997 when we beat them with 12 men after Bobbie Goulding was sent off. Another one going back years is when we beat the Aussies up here 44-2 in 1956, every one of the Saints forwards scored in that game. I remember another Wigan match in 1946-47 when they were unbeaten but we beat them with Jimmy Stott scoring an interception.

There was another Wigan match that stands out not really for the match but for an incident during it. It was in Voll's day when Mick Sullivan was playing for Wigan. Mick Sullivan was marking Voll. The gang I stood with were right on the wall this day. Duggie

140

Greenall came cutting through and gave it to Voll, but Mick Sullivan was waiting for him. Mick Sullivan actually ended up with his hands on the wall proclaiming: "Where the so-and-so has he gone?" Voll was under the sticks.

Finally, if I could take one thing with me from Knowsley Road to the new stadium, it would probably have to be the playing pitch.

Ken Halsall

Ken Halsall is a dedicated Saints supporter. He has records of every Saints game since the war detailing the team that played that day and who scored. He also has a very impressive collection of press cuttings and photographs from throughout the club's history.

I started watching Saints in the 1957-58 season which was van Vollenhoven's first season. I stand on the 25-yard line towards the Eccleston end on the Popular side of the ground but I think you get a good view from all round the ground really.

There are so many games at the ground that stand out for me. One is a third round cup tie in 1961 against Swinton. We were really up against it. Dick Huddart broke down the middle and went under the sticks at the Eccleston end to score a try that won the game for us. I can still see him now going through for that try.

There was also Mal Meninga's last home appearance against Wigan in the Premiership semi-final of 1985 when he gave Phil Ford the hand off. There is still a dent in the pitch where Mal planted him.

And there was a cup tie in 1962 against Huddersfield where it had snowed and it was unsure whether the game was going to be played. We lost and I remember van Vollenhoven flying along the touchline only for Peter Ramsden to take him out completely. Murphy went racing in and ended up getting sent off with Ramsden. There were snowballs flying at Ramsden from the boys' pen.

I think you seem to remember the games more from your school age or in your twenties. They are the games that seem to stand out most for you.

I remember a night match in 1970 against Bradford, we beat them and Kel Coslett kicked 12 out of 12 goals. It was throwing it down, it was a terrible night. Coslett got the world record at the time for successful kicks in a match.

Games against Wigan stand out. In the sixties Wigan had a centre called Alan Davies. Killeen was playing for us and he actually dived over Davies' shoulder to score a try. There are many other tries that stand out. Some of van Vollenhoven's, some of Murphy's.

Little things stand out for me rather than actual matches. At one time, you would go up there and it would be win after win after win. It would be an upset if Saints got beaten.

I remember van Vollenhoven's testimonial. In those days, the players used to get buckets and take them round the crowd for the collection at half-time. It was a Saints-Wigan game, van Vollenhoven went down the tunnel and all the Wigan and Saints players went in the crowd. They did the collection, went into the dressing rooms, had a drink of water or something and then they were back on. They came back on the field ready for the second-half, the ref counted the players and they were one short. It was Billy Boston. He was still in the crowd with the bucket. He climbed over the wall, put the bucket down and the second-half kicked off. He didn't even go and have a drink. Boston and Vollenhoven always seemed good mates. They would walk off the pitch with their arms round each other.

I can remember Saints' first substitute like it was yesterday. We were playing the Aussies. They introduced the subs into Rugby League in 1964-65 but when the Aussies were here in the 1963-64 season they agreed you could have replacements. Australia, at that time, had a bloke called Peter Diamond. He would run through a brick wall and he would give it you. Anyway, Diamond was up against a young Saints player called Mooney and he flattened him. He came off injured and was replaced by Saints' first ever substitute, Arthur Johnson.

Another wonderful memory was the Chris Joynt try against Bradford towards the end of the 2000 season when he scored in the last second to win the game.

The cup game against Hull KR in April 1966 when we were getting beat and Murphy put a bomb up and scored from it is an important memory. One story has the ball bouncing off the wall back to Murph and he scored. But as Murphy said have a look in the *Liverpool Echo* tomorrow. If the ref gives it, it's a try. It was disappointing when Murphy left. I don't know how good the 1966 team was but they'd give today's team a hell of a game. They had a superb pack of forwards with two or three waiting on the sidelines. You had Vollenhoven and Killeen with Killeen being a big-match player. Coslett was another one who would always do it for you in the big games. They were the type of players who thrived on pressure. I don't think any coach can ever coach that into you, you either cope with pressure and perform or you don't. Great players cope with it whether they're 19 or 29, you can see it in them. Good players do the right thing at the right time.

I remember one A team game at Saints. We had a player called Percy Landsberg. They got him from South Africa. He played full-back, centre or stand-off and played in about 30 games for the club. Whoever it was Saints were playing this night had scored a try. The Saints players were behind the posts waiting for the conversion. This Landsberg had massive hands and he stood behind the sticks, the ball was kicked and he caught it in the palm of one hand like it was a cricket ball. I've never seen that before and I've never seen it since.

The Saints-Wigan games have always provided the best atmosphere. Mind you, the Saints-Australia games were always good. When we played them in 1959 at Knowsley Road there must have been about 30,000 there. Then in 1970 Australia had won the World Cup on the Saturday and came to Saints on the Wednesday after. We beat them convincingly. We beat the Aussies in 1956 and all the Saints forwards scored. The atmosphere used to be better in the 1960s because a lot more people used to go.

The player who stands out for me most is definitely Murphy. On playing ability, he is above everyone else. He would have been a great player in any era. He would have been great in the 1930s, would have been great today - just like Ellery Hanley could have played at any time and would have been great. There have been some

143

very good players at Saints like Karalius and van Vollenhoven but I just think Murphy has the edge on them.

I'll be a bit sad when I leave the ground for the last time. It's where I've always walked to the match. I think I'd take the pitch to the new stadium with me if I could. There are not many surfaces better than the one at Knowsley Road.

Tony Bennett

Tony has been watching the side for the past 55 years.

I remember when I was a boy in the mid-1950s, I used to ride my bike to Saints and along with hundreds of other boys would park it at one of three houses next to Saints on Dunriding Lane. You used to pay a few pence for this and would take a sort of raffle ticket to claim your bike after the match.

Another memory from the 1950s and 1960s is that, because there were fewer cars and coaches, there would be thousands of people queuing at Shaw Street station to get on special trains to go to the Wigan match. They did the same thing for Wembley, you would leave at 11p.m. on the Friday and get to London at about 5a.m. on the Saturday, spend the day there watching the game and come back late that night arriving home on Sunday morning.

Over the years, many players have stood out for me. I suppose the first ones would be Duggie Greenall and Tom van Vollenhoven, I would say they are the best centre-wing combination I have ever seen. Duggie was a remarkable player and pound-for-pound was probably the hardest player the game has ever seen.

Voll was one of the greatest try scorers in the game but what people forget is that he was also one of the best defensive wingmen ever. He was very athletic and I have seen him have his ankles tapped, do a forward roll, get up and score. Most people would say that the greatest try he ever scored was the one at Wembley in 1961 but for me the best try I have ever seen an individual player score was the one he got against Hunslet at Odsal in 1958. We eventually won that game 44-22 having been well behind at one stage. It's a pity that one was never recorded.

During this period schoolboy rugby was very strong and it was not uncommon to have crowds in excess of 10,000 for schoolboy finals at Knowsley Road. My own school, St Austins, produced players such as Austin Rhodes, Alex Murphy and the Barrow brothers. The same could be said for many other schools, it's just a pity that we don't have schools playing it now. I'm sure that this is one of the main reasons we are so far behind Australia.

Talking of the Barrow brothers though, you have to mention Frankie. As well as being an excellent player he was also a character and there are many stories told about him on the after dinner circuit. One of these concerns Billy Thompson, the ex-referee who was refereeing a Saints versus Salford game. He was well known for his short-back-and-sides haircut. He recounts that at one stage in the game a Salford player broke away and only had Frankie to beat who promptly brought him down with a stiff arm. He says he was about to send him off when Frankie said: "Bloody hell Billy, where did you get your hair cut?" He never did send him off.

A game that stands out for me was when we beat the Australian tourists in 1956. It was the best game Josh Gaskell played. One of the Australian forwards that day broke through and only had Glyn Moses to beat. Everyone in the ground could see that he was out to flatten Glyn. Moses just stood his ground and then hit him with his shoulder knocking him to the ground, mind you I have seen him do that to many people including Billy Boston.

I'd have to say that Alex Murphy is simply the best rugby player I have ever seen. It was obvious from his early school days that Alex was going to become a great player. He could side-step on a sixpence, had blistering acceleration and his speed over 40 yards was incredible. He was an all-round sportsman excelling at football and cricket.

From today's players I'd have to pick out Sean Long. He too has great acceleration, you can see this when he spots a gap and seems to go into overdrive. He is also very good defensively and his goal kicking has improved a great deal over the past few years. His work-rate is such that he must be one of the fittest players in the game today. Keiron Cunningham is another world-class player. Not only does he have the strength and agility to evade the opposition, he also has the speed to get himself to the try-line over a long distance. He is also probably the best defensive forward in the game today.

You would have to go a long way to better some of the tries that Anthony Sullivan has scored over the years and there is no finer sight in rugby than Sully in full flight.

I did say that the finest individual try I have ever seen was the Tom van Vollenhoven try against Hunslet.

The best team try I have seen has to be Chris Joynt's against Bradford in the play-offs of 2000. You had the occasion equal to that of a cup game, the clock on the big screen ticking down and Saints some 70 yards from the Bradford try- line when the move started. I think Matthew Elliott's disappearing act as we crossed the line sums it all up.

Without a doubt, the best atmosphere at Knowsley Road is when we play Wigan. There have been games against other clubs that have equalled it but, for sheer consistency, it has to be Saints versus Wigan.

The best Saints side I have seen is probably the 1966 side that won all four cups, although since Super League started we have had some good ones as the number of trophies we have won shows.

I always used to stand on the terraces until some seven years ago when I went into the stand. I have to say that the view from the stand is far better although you do lose some of the atmosphere.

One of the funniest things I have seen on the ground was when Shane Cooper hid the ball under his jersey when playing Widnes. I have a friend who supports Widnes who still complains about that.

There are many memories of Knowsley Road but I do think it is time to move on. What proved this for me was when they were looking for a ground that looked like Old Trafford in the 1950s and 1960s for the filming of the George Best movie and they chose Knowsley Road.

Mick Gill

Mick's main memories of watching Saints are in the Vollenhoven era. Voll was a favourite of Mick and he owns the training jersey that Voll used to wear at the club.

I have watched Saints for years, from when all the good players played in the 1950s. I first went when I was about eight years old.

I remember there being a little, old battered fence running around the pitch when I first started going. The Kop was just a hill then. I used to stand on the halfway line of the Popular side.

Voll was the best winger I have ever seen. I saw his first game against Leeds and I saw his last game against Warrington. I remember his debut in 1957, Leeds kicked the ball over the Saints line and Tommy was standing over it. He didn't pick it up and Leeds came through and scored. He hadn't quite got to grips with League rules then. At the end of the game though he scored a cracking try. He was a gentleman on and off the pitch, he was absolutely superb. He never got sent off. In the 1958-59 season he scored 62 tries for Saints. He always went down the wing, he would never cut inside. He had blistering pace and a tremendous hand-off. His defensive work has never been equalled since. He was tremendous in defence on the opposite wing as well as his own. You would always know when Tommy was in full flight because his head would drop slightly to one side. He could easily play in today's game.

Murphy was a good player of course, as was the 'Wild Bull of the Pampas' Vince Karalius. Vinty was a marvellous ball player. He had hands like shovels and would hold the ball in one hand. It was a bigger, heavier ball back in those days as well. He would roll his sleeves up, he was very muscular. He used to look after Murphy. He even told one scrum-half: "Don't come round that side of the scrum again," after he tackled him.

One of Voll's centres Keith Northey had a side-step like a wicket keeper where he would jump in the air. I thought Tommy Bishop was one of the best scrum halves we had. He was a different player to Alex, shorter and stockier. He would take any forward on. Len

Killeen was an excellent player even though he didn't have great pace. He was a great goal-kicker. The speed men we had at the club were amazing. Voll, Prinsloo, Carlton, Large and Murphy over 35 yards was like lightening. There were certainly some good forwards in the 1950s and 1960s. I thought Jim Measures was a good running forward with plenty of pace. Dick Huddart was another class forward.

Voll's training jersey was given to me by a chap I worked with at British Sidac. He had got it through a friend-of-a-friend type of thing.

All the Wigan games were very good in those days. Mind you, all the top games were good, such as when we played Leeds and so on. There were a lot more good teams around then than there is today. Most teams had at least one good winger. There are very few good wingers about nowadays. Even the smallest of teams like Liverpool City had a good winger.

Johnny Stopford was a great player, he played on the wing for Swinton. He scored two hat-tricks against Voll, one of the very few who did that. He was only small but exceptionally fast. He was one of the fastest in Rugby League.

Other opposing players who stand out are the likes of the Wigan players Mick Sullivan and Billy Boston and later on Frank Carlton who went from Saints to Wigan. He was an excellent winger. Fred 'Punchy' Griffiths, the Wigan full-back, was a good player as were the Fox brothers at Wakefield. One of the best centres I have ever seen was Eric Ashton.

Most games then were very good to watch. Of course, it wasn't six tackles then, you had possession until you lost it. Conditions were different to what they are now. Today, I feel there is far too much kicking when a team is in their opponents 25-yard area. You should be able to score in your opponents 25 by passing the ball. The 25-yard area at either end should be for playing rugby not football. Don't get me wrong I think today's game is good and exciting but they should just cut down on the attacking kicking.

It'll be a bit nostalgic when the Knowsley Road ground has gone. There are a lot of memories there.

Paul Bennett

Paul is a Saints supporter who not only takes his young son Thomas to the game but has also involved his wife Jackie in supporting Saints. He has been watching the side since the mid-seventies.

I've been watching the side for about 25 years now. The players who were playing then were the likes of Les Jones, Roy Mathias and Geoff Pimblett. A game that stands out for me early on, when I was very young, was when we beat Dewsbury 72-12 just after Christmas. I remember we were near the Dewsbury directors and one of them looked like Father Christmas. That coupled with the fact that we were winning easily meant I got over-excited. That was when I used to stand by the restaurant. I've watched games from a few different parts of the ground. You seem to have spells where you'll have a season standing here, a season standing there. I currently stand with my wife Jackie on the 25-yard line of the Popular side towards the Edington end. Jackie is from Liverpool, she had never really seen Rugby League before, she came to one Saints game and now she is hooked. You get a good view, you get some of the atmosphere where we stand without being too much involved with the 'Scaff' - officially known as the Popular Side.

One of my favourite players early on was Roy Mathias but that could have something to do with the fact that my uncle, who I stood with, was one of Roy's best mates. I remember the crowd at the time would scream at Roy to thump the opposition winger and if he didn't they would call him all sorts. 'Slasher', as he was known, and Les Jones scored some tries between them.

We've always done well for hookers here. In the recent past we've had Graham Liptrot, Paul Groves, Bernard Dwyer and now of course Keiron Cunningham, all very good players. I used to think Neil Holding was good because he was all commitment. It's like that now with Sean Long. They're the type of player who will make mistakes but still keep plugging away. Saints fans get annoyed at players if they see someone with the talent who doesn't appear to be trying. The supporters would love to have the skill of the players so they could go out and do it. Supporters would try to run through a wall for Saints. Sean Long works very hard at his game.

The best side I've seen at Saints is the team who won back-to-back titles in 1999 and 2000 and went on to be crowned World Club Champions in 2001.

A strange thing I remember happened in the 2000 season when Tommy Martyn scored a freak try against Wakefield. Sean Long had gone to kick a penalty, he missed the kick but Tommy chased the ball and caught it and dived over.

I think the funniest thing I've seen at the ground was one match in the early 1980s and it was a really foggy night. You couldn't see anything, we heard cheers as Saints had scored. We asked Saints winger Kevin Meadows who had scored and even he had no idea.

I think it would have been more of a wrench to leave our ground if we had been the first team to do it. Seeing other teams moving homes has made it easier I think. I'll miss the familiarity of the place. Knowsley Road is the place you go to watch rugby when you're at home.

Mike Critchley

Mike is a sports journalist who has been watching Saints for more than 20 years. He is the sports editor of the St Helens Star.

I've been watching Saints since 1978. My first game was after the 1978 Wembley Cup Final where we got beaten by Leeds. My first actual game at Knowsley Road wasn't a Saints game, it was England versus Wales. It was a game that had been postponed from Swansea. I was never really into Saints but I got swept into it when the team came home from Wembley on the bus. The bus came down Dentons Green Lane and I remember waving at Bill Francis and he waved back. I thought: "This can't be bad". So my dad took me to the next game which was the England and Wales match. England tonked Wales and there were a few Saints players involved in the match. Geoff Pimblett made his only international appearance for England. The Welsh side had Bill Francis, Roy Mathias and an ex-Saint in the form of John Mantle. Sully's dad, Clive Sullivan was also playing for them. It was great but I just kicked myself that it was May and I would have to wait until September for the season to start to see my next game.

My first Saints games

My first Saints game was Leeds in the John Player Trophy. It was on a Saturday and it was a televised game. It sticks out for a daft reason really. I had forgotten my glasses so the only person who stood out for me was Roy Mathias because he was big and closest to the touchline. Saints won and I remember running on and patting Mathias on the back. You think of wingmen as not so big, but fast. Mathias was a big bloke though. I would say he was probably my first hero really. He'd get the ball and put his head down, he was really fiery. I only saw him at the end of his career, I'd have loved to have seen him in his pomp.

When I first started going, I always used to stand at the Edington end. The first season, I spent most of the time looking around to be honest. It was part of my learning curve in the game. I used to take my programme home and learn the positions. I'd spent all the seventies watching football like you do when you're a kid. All the other kids used to follow Saints or Liverpool so to be a bit of a rebel I supported Leeds United. Obviously, the Edington end in the late seventies used to be where crowd trouble occurred which was fascinating for me to see.

In the 1980s I always used to stand in the paddock, I loved the paddock. They used to have the coaches dugouts on that side in those days and I used to enjoy having a good shout at the opposition coaches and subs. I remember after one "needling" session one of the Halifax coaching staff threw the water sponge bag at me. I loved it there.

Then I started going on the popular side when Meninga came. That was it for me, from then on I've stood there ever since.

Soap Aid

One summer in the late 1970s, believe it or not there was professional wrestling on the ground. The main event was Big Daddy taking on Mighty John Quinn. The ring was in front of a packed main stand. There was a great atmosphere and my voice was hoarse at the end of it. There is a St Helens connection with Daddy because his mother-in-law lived in Greenfield Road. There was also a Rugby League connection as he used to play for Dewsbury. Of course, the wrestling was all staged but it was all right for a laugh, especially when an elderly women launched an apple core at Mighty John Quinn.

Another recollection I have is the ill-fated Soap Aid held at the ground in the summer of 1986. I remember afterwards someone said: "You can never hold anything in St Helens without there being trouble." I went to the event and people just got plastered even though there was supposed to be no drink inside. I remember Anita Dobson, Angie from *Eastenders*, got up on stage and shouted: "Good morning Liverpool" for which she was roundly booed. It was only salvaged by the chap who played Pete Beale saying: "This is St Helens and we hope you get to Wembley in the Challenge Cup, we'd love to see you down in London in May." He was actually right because for the first time in nine years we went to Wembley the following May, all thanks to Pete Beale! I also remember Fish from Marillion breaking off his set to state that: "This is a concert not a battleground" because there was so much fighting taking place. The Grange Hill cast sang *Just say no*. The mayor at the time was chasing after them trying to get their autographs all day. Percy Sugden from Corrie gave a rendition on the banjo. Also, Helen Shapiro sang because she was in *Albion Market* at the time. Ricky Tomlinson, now of *The Royle Family*, was compering it. He was a brilliant speaker because he just laid into Margaret Thatcher. They lost money on the event, it was a wash-out, I reckon there were only about 2,000 there on the pitch. The stage was set up at the clubhouse end of the ground. I think the day was Andy Lynch's idea. He was one of the writers for *Brookside* at the time. It was his idea obviously after

Band Aid and Fashion Aid to do an event with soap stars and to hold it at Knowsley Road because he was a local lad. It was mentioned on *Breakfast BBC News* but apart from that didn't get much coverage.

In later life, during my role as reporter, I interviewed Ian McNabb from the Icicle Works who had performed at Soap Aid. He still remembers getting thrown down the stairs of The Fleece by the bouncers. If the event had been anywhere else, I probably wouldn't have gone. I was just happy to be inside the ground.

The last game of the season at the ground used to be the Eric Bromilow Cup, the amateur competition. I always used to go to that as it was your last look at the ground for another two or three months.

Best players

One Saints player who stands out for me would have to be Meninga. If you look at the 1984-85 season, a ton of Aussies came over to Britain. Leeds signed a lot of them including people like Eric Grothe yet these players did nothing. They didn't have half the impact that Meninga had. The other thing was that Meninga came to a club that hadn't won anything for years. A lot of us had grown up and seen the club win nothing. When you live through something like that, any successes that follow the first success you witness even if they are bigger and aren't quite the same.

It was the Lancashire Cup that we first won, a trophy we don't even have in the game anymore. All the way through the October of that season, the Saints fans were walking on air. Billy Benyon had got the team playing a particular style of rugby the previous two seasons. They were a team of young lads who were very talented but didn't really have the firepower up front to allow us to play football. We didn't really have a forceful pack when Meninga was here. But the thing was, opposition teams would very often put three men on him meaning more space for Neil Holding, Chris Arkwright or Harry Pinner. You had a winger like Barrie Ledger to finish moves as well. Meninga allowed us the room to play football and he also gave us a confidence boost. Peter Gorley that season was phenomenal.

153

The next person I'd pick out is a coach, Shaun McRae. He probably doesn't get enough credit for what he did for the club. He took us to Super League success and two Challenge Cups.

I think out of the hundreds of opposition players I've seen at the ground, you're looking at Andy Gregory and Ellery Hanley as the ones who stand out the most. I remember the first try I saw Hanley score against us at Knowsley Road. He was playing for Bradford and was 30 yards out on the left-hand side of the ground. He ran the full width of the pitch sideways and no-one laid a finger on him and he scored in front of where the old scoreboard used to be in the corner. He marked himself out as a player who was a bit special. When he developed his physical attributes, he was awesome. I remember a quote that was attributed to Chris Arkwright that went: "Hanley's got the hardest head I've ever hit".

Gavin Miller is another one who stands out for me. He played loose-forward for Hull KR. He ripped us apart that awful night at Knowsley Road where Saints were knocked out of the Challenge Cup. With it being our Meninga season, we thought it was going to be our year in 1985. Our hearts sunk when we lost that night.

Unforgettable games

As for games, I remember in the early 1980s we played Hull in the Challenge Cup at home. Hull must have brought about 5,000 fans and they completely occupied the Popular side. Everywhere you looked was black and white. They were the team to beat at the time. Paul Newlove's dad was playing for them at stand-off, he had a cracking pair of hands. I remember Gorley going off injured for us and Neil Holding dislocating his shoulder. All you heard was *Old Faithful* all afternoon. We won but it was a roller coaster of a game. I felt sick coming out of the ground, I was emotionally drained. That was a great game but all the Hull games were special back then. They had a great team and they brought the fans with them.

It's strange really but it seems to be the defeats that I remember most over the years at Knowsley Road. I still have nightmares over the day Featherstone knocked us out of the Challenge Cup at home in

1983. It was Saturday on *Grandstand*, we had beaten Leeds in the previous round. It made it worse that it was televised because everyone else saw what happened. It was horrible losing on a Saturday. In those days, there was nothing else to do on a Sunday but go to the game. If you had lost the day before, there was nothing open on a Sunday and all you could do was sulk. I was standing in the paddock that day and John Gilbert's late try seemed to be played out in slow motion. We thought we were going to Wembley that year and all the Hull players were in the stand to watch us because they had heard we were the team to beat.

Fev just stretched a wall of muscle across the field and Saints played into their hands by driving it in with the forwards. They knocked the living daylights out of us. Eventually, Roy Haggerty scored and we thought their resistance was broken. We were all happy then. Just a few minutes from the end, Keith Bell got the ball on his own 25, shimmied, well I'm not sure Keith Bell could shimmy but you know what I mean, put a long ball out and John Gilbert ended up under the posts. I remember the Featherstone fans going absolutely berserk. That was it, it was awful. They went on to Wembley and won. That was the last bit of real joy that Featherstone have had on or off the pitch. With hindsight, I really wouldn't begrudge them that.

Losing to Wigan in 1984 was awful. They were just making their way out of the doldrums. You need two rival clubs. Hull fed off Hull KR as we fed off Wigan, the thing was Wigan took it too far! It had thrown it down all day. There were 20,000 on the ground and you could hardly move. I never thought I would see the ground so packed. Like I said, the rain had lashed down. What I could never work out is why they had played a curtain raiser before the game which was one of the most stupid decisions ever made.

Wigan had big, dour forwards and we had a light, mobile pack with the likes of Round, Gorley and Platt. If it had been dry, we would have won easily. Anyway, Barrie Ledger scored a cracking try that day. Late on, we were leading. It was the last tackle and Clive Griffiths, in an unbelievable display of ineptitude in my opinion, came off his wing and kicked to the side of the field he had vacated. The kick failed to reach touch and Wigan scored.

People who left Knowsley Road early that day were going home thinking we had won because we had held the lead right until the end. I walked home that day, gutted. I couldn't go straight home because I knew I wouldn't be able to eat my tea. I bumped into an old bloke by the cemetery. He'd left about seven minutes from the end, he probably thought we'd got it in the bag and being old decided to beat the rush. He said to me: "What score did it finish up cock?" I told him we had lost 16-7. He just couldn't believe it and started crying. It brought it home to me how much it means to people. That probably ruined his weekend. He was an old bloke who had lived through the war and other hard times, yet Saints losing reduced him to tears. That bloke may not have been alive to see our long awaited success of 1996.

The day we beat Warrington at home in 1996 to win the Super League obviously stands out for me. But in terms of an electric atmosphere, the game I'd pick is the 1984 Lancashire Cup semi-final at home to Leigh. It was the Wednesday after the Sunday when Meninga had made his debut against Castleford. There were about 10,000 there and a great atmosphere. Veivers had a stormer, every time he had the ball the crowd was yelling "Veivers, Veivers". It was superb to win that because it meant we had reached a final.

The year we beat Wigan in the Lancashire Cup semi-final in 1991 at home was memorable. The atmosphere was superb, it was a night game and we were very much the underdogs. Paul Forber scored very early on for us and we went on to win comfortably. Mike Riley scored another cracker in the second half. We went on to beat Rochdale in the final.

Once the ground has gone, it will feel awful really. Once you leave it, it's not going to feel the same, you're not going to have the same memories of "that's the corner where Mathias scored", "I remember that bit", "I was stood there when this happened". When you're at a match, you do replay flashbacks in your head. It's not the same when you're in a different place. I feel strongly that the new stadium should have a provision for standing otherwise people who have been going to the game together for years may not be able to sit together if any of them turn up late or whatever. It's not just the concrete and turf that's getting tossed away, it's a lot of our memories as well. The one thing I won't miss is the appalling PA system that they've had in the past.

The one thing I'll miss most about Knowsley Road is the terraces. Silly little things like the old turnstiles which if you judged them wrong, they'd catch you in the crotch.

As a kid, all the exotic smells such as wintergreen, cigar smoke from the stand and stale beer from under the stand. All clichés of course but all true.

Kevin

Kevin has been watching the team for more than 20 years.

I got my first season ticket in 1980, I've still got it actually, it cost seven pounds and had a green cover. Since then, I've been following the side home and away. My first actual visit to Knowsley Road to watch the side was in 1976 when I was eight years old. We were playing Widnes and I can remember it was freezing cold and I also remember looking at the old scoreboard. It was an old wooden scoreboard with a clock on it. It's now the police control room. There seemed to be a big crowd there that day because I remember going for a cup of tea and I couldn't find my dad.

When I first started going, I used to go in the Paddock which is under the main stand. You used to have to pay 10p to get into the Paddock on top of the admission fee. I used to sit on the wall and one of my earliest memories of that time was watching Kevin Meadows running past me down the wing.

When I got a bit older, I moved onto the Scaff which is of course on the halfway line. Now, I stand at the Edington end of the ground. You can have a good banter with the majority of away fans.

My favourite part of the ground is actually the steps in the corner between the main stand and Edington end of the ground. You walk up the steps and you can see the whole of the pitch and ground. You can see how many people are there and what kind of atmosphere it's going to be.

The players

The Saints players who stand out for me? Well, first of all it has to be Mal Meninga without a doubt. The best player ever, he had so much power and strength, he virtually carried the side that season. Other players stand out for me though like Peter Gorley, I always remember shouting: "Someone back up Gorley" as he was a very good second- rower from Cumbria who did well for the club. I always used to like Barrie Ledger, our winger. He had pace and scored a lot of tries for the club. One of my all-time favourite players is 'Coops', our former captain Shane Cooper. He had a great rugby brain, had a good dummy and would tackle non-stop. He was the brains behind the team of the early 1990s.

Then there was the best prop I've seen at Saints, Kevin Ward. When we signed him from Castleford, I thought he's getting on a bit but he was superb for the club. He was the last of the real prop forwards in my book.

You can't take anything away from Bobbie Goulding though can you? He won us the double in 1996 with his organising and clever play. Without him, we were lost. He could put players through massive gaps with his clever passing.

Out of the current squad, I'd have to pick out Paul Newlove. He has scored a lot of tries for the club and can win a game for you in an instant.

Out of the opposition players I've seen, the two who stand out for me most are Shaun Edwards and Ellery Hanley - the strength of Hanley and the skill of Edwards. I hated both of them because they played for Wigan, but even I have to admit as a Saints fan that they were both superb players. Also, Martin Offiah when he was at Widnes and first making a name for himself was excellent, you couldn't give him a yard or he'd be away.

Games I remember

The games that stand out most for me are any of the Wigan games, especially when we beat the pie eaters. The 2000 win when we beat them 38-14 was one of the better ones, as was the 1992 game where we battered them 41-6, I still remember Sonny Nickle diving in at the corner and the supporters going wild. The Hull and Hull KR games when they were doing well in the mid-eighties were good as well. We always seemed to paste them when they came to Knowsley Road. They were good teams and used to bring loads of support making for a good atmosphere.

I remember in 1986 when we played Carlisle in a cup competition and beat them 112-0. I was sitting in the stand that day with a couple of my mates. I like close games and when I went to the Carlisle game I remember thinking it was going to be very one-sided and boring. We got to 50-0, 60-0, then when we got to 80-0 you think God, we could actually score 100 points here. I remember telling the people around me that a century was on the cards and they just laughed because it was rarely heard of in Rugby League. I think it was actually Barrie Ledger who got the 100 up with a try. There wasn't much of a crowd but they went wild when the 100 got put on the scoreboard. To score 100 points in a game was a real achievement. At the end of the match, everyone in the stand rose to their feet to give Saints a standing ovation.

The Sheffield game in 1996, the week before we won the title stands out as well. The weather was nice, the atmosphere was good, there was a good team spirit at the club and David Howes was making a real effort promoting the side. There were 9,021 fans on that night and they were all home fans. We played fantastic rugby as well, one of the best performances you'll see from any side.

I think another thing that helps is that you've got three sides under cover at Saints which amplifies the crowd's shouting and cheering. If you go to places like Hull and you're out in the open, the noise isn't the same. Away fans at Knowsley Road though go to the Edington end under cover and it adds to the atmosphere.

Speaking of atmosphere, the games that provide the best atmosphere are definitely the Wigan games, well until five minutes have gone and we're getting pasted that is. They are nerve-wracking games because, to be honest, you always feel that you're going to get pasted. Mind you, there's nothing worse than the feeling in your stomach when you're beating Wigan at home by a couple of points and you just know Wigan are going to snatch it. I'd sooner be getting thrashed than losing a game to them in the final seconds. More recently, the Leeds and Bradford games have created a good atmosphere because they're both doing well and they bring a lot of supporters.

The funniest thing I saw at the ground is a bit cruel actually. There was a lad standing near me and he jumped up when Saints scored but lost his balance and went flying down the terracing. All the away fans had a good chuckle at that. He was uninjured, just a bit embarrassed. I also think it's funny when one of your mates gets the players mixed up and shouts the wrong name, you can have a laugh at their expense.

I'll be disappointed to leave the ground for the last time but I'm afraid you've got to move on. I wasn't very keen on the idea at first but I've got more used to it now and after all you've always got your memories.

The thing I'll miss most about the ground is standing on the terracing with the lads shouting and having a laugh. In the new place, most of us will be sitting down and I do think you lose something when you do that. So, yeah, I'll miss standing on the terracing, having a laugh, a good shout and a moan. Believe it or not, it has been said that us Saints supporters can be a bit critical at times.

I think it would be wonderful to take the terracing from the Edington and scoreboard ends of the ground to the new stadium and plonk them behind each set of posts. That way, we could stand up on the terracing while the rest of the ground is seated.

I'd like a crush barrier from the ground for my back garden. I'd also like that sign in the paddock that says: "St Helens RFC". I'd like a bit of the turf from the Edington end of the ground also.

Linda Edwards

Linda has been a Saints fan for 20 years and used to work at the club as a cleaner. She lives near the ground and is currently on the committee of the Independent Saints Supporters' Association.

My first memory that comes to mind of watching Saints is fainting during a game. I was pregnant at the time and I just went down, embarrassing my husband Stan in the process.

I stand at the clubhouse end of the ground in front of the restaurant. I have to say though that my favourite part of the ground is definitely the playing field.

Out of all the Saints players I've seen I'd say Neil Holding stands out along with Phil Veivers. I always remember way back Kel Coslett kicking a goal from the halfway line. More recently, I'd have to say Bobbie Goulding and Keiron Cunningham have impressed me.

As for the opposition players who've graced Knowsley Road over the years I'd have to say Lee Crooks was a great player. I also think that Iestyn Harris is a wonderful footballer.

I think one game that stands out for me was the first game of the 2000 season where we got beaten by Bradford, it turned out to be Ellery Hanley's last game in charge. There were all sorts going on behind the scenes so I remember that night.

Most of the Wigan games stand out obviously. I think whenever Warrington come to Knowsley Road there is a good atmosphere. It's good when Bradford come because they bring so many supporters which also helps make a good atmosphere.

One moment I won't forget is when I went onto the pitch on behalf of ISSA to present a cake to Saints coach Ian Millward for his birthday. It was televised on Sky and I was shaking like a leaf.

I will be very emotional when I leave Knowsley Road for the last time. All the memories and people that you associate with the place will be gone, it's unbelievable really.

The Knowsley Road ghost

When I worked as a cleaner at the ground I would clean under the main stand, where the bar used to be and also the changing rooms. There was a rumour going round that there was a ghost at the ground. I remember one day in winter I was going in to clean under the main stand. It was very dark and you had to walk halfway down a corridor until you got to the light switch. I had to go to the very far end, the far changing room to clean it. I went in, got halfway down and heard a noise. I looked around but there was nothing there. I opened the changing room door, it was pitch black and a body appeared in front of me and I screamed. It was Neil Holding. He used to torment me like mad when I worked there.

The thing I'll miss most about the ground is the people that I stand with. When we go to the new ground I'll have to sit down. I sometimes stand with people who work away from St Helens and unless we meet up before a game at the new ground we're not going to be able to sit together. I think you'll lose a lot of the atmosphere that you have at Knowsley Road.

If I could take one thing with me to the new ground I would take the same pitch because it is fantastic.

There's one souvenir I'd love from the ground. I've been in the boardroom and they've got this big picture of Bobbie Goulding on the open top bus coming back from Wembley. He's wearing a Saints scarf and it's my scarf that I threw to him in Kirkland Street when the bus went down there. I'd love that photo or at least a copy of it.

John Yates

John is currently Sports Editor of the St Helens Reporter and provides match reports on all Saints games. He is a former editor of the Rugby Leaguer and is also secretary of Burscough Cricket Club.

From 1980 to about 1989 I had a dual role, I was Sports Editor of the *St Helens Reporter* and Editor of the *Rugby Leaguer*. I brought the *Rugby Leaguer* out of the dark ages by introducing colour.

My background is really in football and cricket but for the past 20 years I've been covering Saints matches.

Looking back to when I first started covering matches, I remember Harry Pinner, the captain of the side and also Barrie Ledger, a wingman who could score tries from anywhere. They were only part time players then but the side had some good players. Roy Haggerty, for me, personified everything you wanted a Saints player to be. He was tough, rugged and he would give you his all for 80 minutes. Harry Pinner though, was the lynchpin of the side. If the opposition let Harry play, that was it. I don't think the club has ever had a better ball handler than him.

Then of course there was Mal Meninga. He was a sort of Adonis at the club. He is the first Rugby League player to come to this county and get full page publicity in the broadsheet Sunday newspapers. He made such an impact on the town.

A reporter's matchday

A normal Saints matchday for a reporter means that before you leave the office you make sure you've got your pens, paper and that your cassette recorder is working. When you get into the ground your first stop is a little canteen under the tunnel where all the press meet. There's a few ladies there to serve us with cups of tea and that. Then it's up to the press box to cover the match. You have to pick out the highlights and try to find an angle. If there isn't an angle, you've got to hope that someone will say something in the press conference afterwards to give you an angle. There is always a press conference after the game. The coaches are there and sometimes one or two of the players - perhaps someone has scored a hat trick that day, they will attend. It's all well organised. Dave Burke, the club's PR man does quite a good job. It is work but at the same time it's enjoyment. There is stress though as you've got to work to tight deadlines. I've not got the same pressure as some of the national newspaper reporters. They've got to file copy [send in their report] as the match is taking place. The deadlines are so tight now that some of the nationals are asking for the opening paragraph of the piece 15 minutes before the end of the match. That's impossible because the result could very easily change in the last quarter of an hour. The problem with the coverage of the game today is that copy is filed to a London office rather than a Manchester one. In a London office, the chances are the person there doesn't know anything about Rugby League and that's why you see pictures of players with a different player's name on the caption. Unless you drop on someone with a bit of Rugby League knowledge, you're banging your head against a brick wall.

The easiest person to interview during my time covering Saints had to be Shaun McRae, without a shadow of a doubt. He is a gentleman to start with. No matter when you wanted to see him, he would find time for you. You would only have to ask him one question and he would just keep talking about the club. He is the perfect coach to interview. Believe it or not, some of the players are a bit frightened of doing interviews. Chris Joynt hates being interviewed by the press. He knows he's got to do it and he's getting a bit more used to it now. I always found Bobbie Goulding very easy to interview.

In terms of actual skill, I think the Regal Trophy semi-final at home to Warrington where we beat them 80-0 in 1995 was amazing. The performance that night was perfection. That was a game where the match report just flowed off my computer.

I'm a person for progress and I think the club has got to move ground. If you don't move with the times, you'll just get left behind.

Ste Rigby

Ste has been a Saints supporter for more than 20 years. He works for a local printing firm who produce Saints' match programmes.

I have been watching Saints for about 23 years, I can't remember exactly who we played when I went to my first game. I do remember though that I was about six or seven years old. Players such as Les Jones, Geoff Pimblett and Roy Mathias were playing. Games were played on Saturdays then and my uncle took me to the match because my dad said he was busy. When I got to the match, my dad was standing in front of us. He took me to all the games after that as I would not swallow the "I'm busy" excuse.

I'd say my favourite part of the ground is behind the sticks at the tunnel end of the ground as I stood there for years and years.

As for my involvement with the production of the programme, I basically just put ink onto paper. It's not very exciting most of the time but it is a pleasure to print if you have beaten Wigan the week before. One thing that does happen on a regular basis is that because of my involvement, people tend to hold me fully responsible for any mistakes contained within.

Older people might say players are not as good as they were in their day but that statement is bull. I'd say the following Saints players have stood out for me the most. Kevin Ward who is without doubt the best prop I have ever seen. Then of course there is Mal Meninga. The best player in the world playing for Saints? Surely not. Bobbie Goulding may have caused a bit of trouble off the park but when we won the league and cup double in 1996, he was outstanding. Then there is Keiron Cunningham. There is nothing better than seeing a St Helens lad play for Saints and be the best in the world at his position.

As for opposing players who stood out for me at Knowsley Road, I've got to mention Ellery Hanley. I called him a few names in the past but he was a class player. There was also Martin Offiah, I always thought when he lost a bit of speed he would be crap. However, when he had pace, he was brilliant. I feel sick saying this about Wigan players.

My stand-out game at the ground would have to be beating Wigan in 1997 in the Challenge Cup with 12 men. It was the first real sign that the tide was turning and the Wigan fans knew it. That match also provided a brilliant atmosphere.

I'll feel sad when I leave the ground for the last time. Taking the trip to Knowsley Road has been part of my life for a long time but progress is progress.

The thing I'll miss most about the ground is definitely the atmosphere because when you are standing, with 9 or 10,000 there, it can feel quite full. Can this be reproduced in an all seater stadium? I hope so.

The one thing I'd take to the new ground from Knowsley Road is the pitch as it is better than my lawn.

James Michael

James has been a Saints fan from the early 1980s up to the present day and here recollects his time at Saints as a youngster.

You should have seen me. I raced past one lad in Halifax colours, my pace leaving him for dead, another was coming across from the left but I stepped him and continued on. My legs were pumping, there was no one to stop me, I made it to the posts and... asked Mal Meninga for his autograph.

Yes, as a little 'un I was one of the many who would sprint onto the pitch at the end of the game to ask for autographs. The most amazing on-pitch autographing session I saw was Alex Murphy's first game back as coach in late 1987. He was surrounded by literally hundreds of little kids clutching their programmes. I had waited ages and just as I got to the front the security man alongside Alex said: "That's enough, he'll be here next home game" but Alex still reached out for my programme and signed it.

You think getting served at last orders is tough, you should have tried dodging through the demented throng to get Meninga's signature at a home game. In fact, no matter what the score was, the last 10 minutes of any game of the 1984-85 season were spent plotting the direct route to Meninga and keeping a close eye on where he was stood. I prayed for the hooter to go with Mal tackled in front of where I was but it never happened. In fact, it's a miracle that we waited for the hooter to go at all. Imagine the fury in the national papers as Rugby League suffers a pitch invasion not from hooligans but tearaway seven-year-olds determined to get an autograph or sock tie-ups. I did have good taste though in my autograph collecting. I still have programmes bearing the signature of the Hull Kiwis of Gary Kemble, James Leulai and Dane O'Hara, the great Wigan imports of Brett Kenny and Chikka Ferguson. I don't think that would happen now, a Saints kid asking a Wigan player for an autograph but what can I say? I was young and impressionable and needed the playground kudos of having an Aussie international's autograph.

Chris

Chris has been watching the side from the 1970s to present day.

The first thing I remember about going to Saints with my dad when I was very young is that it was always freezing. I always remember my dad putting me under the massive jacket he had and lifting me on the wall. The wall had pebbles on it so it wasn't very comfortable. I can also remember my legs going numb, when I used to jump on the pitch at the end of the game with all the other kids I couldn't run properly at first because I couldn't get my legs going. I remember jumping on the pitch after some games during winter and the pitch would be rock solid. I used to watch from the clubhouse end of the ground in those days, in the boys' pen.

I remember one televised game when I was about 14 and I had a bet with my mates for 50p each that I would run on the pitch. It was a Saturday afternoon game and I wanted to get on telly. As the players came out of the tunnel, I jumped over the wall onto the turf. They used to leave the ball on the middle of the pitch then. I sprinted across to it, picked it up, Jeff Heaton came running over, I passed the ball to him and ran back to where I had been standing. I jumped back over the wall and they all had to give me 50p each.

In later years, I used to stand on the 25 on the main stand side of the ground. One of my friends at the time was Gary Connolly who was then playing for Saints. When Saints came out, they had a spell of throwing little plastic rugby balls into the crowd. We used to see Gary in the pub in the week before the game and he would always know we would be standing on the 25. So, he always used to try and throw one of these balls to us. We never got one though. You could see when Gary came out of the tunnel he would be looking for us and laughing.

I'd say the Edington is my favourite part of the ground because you can have good Craic with the away supporters.

Neil Holding stands out for me out of all the players I've seen at Saints. He was very unfortunate with injuries. I can't comment on Meninga because I was working in France the season he played. Pinner was a good player. Jeff Heaton was a good scrum-half in the sixties and seventies. Today, you'd have to say Sean Long really wouldn't you? But as a bloke who can win a game for you, I'd go for Newlove. He can just do something to turn a game for you and he's one of the few centres who can go the full length of the pitch.

As for opposition players I've seen at the ground I have to say 'The King'. Ellery Hanley was head and shoulders above the rest. The amount of times he ripped us to bits was unbelievable. Shaun Edwards had some good games against us and Dean Bell was another player who stands out. Even Joe Lydon wasn't a bad player. Hanley was ahead of his time. He was at a standard that the Australians reached a couple of years later. He was quick, had great upper body strength and could offload the ball with three men on him.

Any game where we beat Wigan stands out for me, the atmosphere is always incredible. One moment that sticks in my mind is when Jarrod McCracken tackled Bell and knocked him out. He actually dragged Bell to his feet to play the ball and Bell just collapsed. I can still see that now. The game that will stick in my memory away from the Wigan encounters is the Bradford game in 2000 when Chris Joynt scored that last-second try. I bet if they tried to recreate that try in training, one of them would drop it. Another one was where Paul Forber scored a late try for us to beat New Zealand at home in 1989.

The best try I saw scored at the ground was Les Quirk's against Hull in February 1991. We were losing in the last few minutes and Les went down the Popular side touchline to score the winner at the Edington end of the ground.

I think the strangest atmosphere there was when we played Hull in 1999, the Sunday after coach Ellery Hanley was suspended. It felt like everybody was together against the directors - everybody supporting Saints and wanting Ellery to be reinstated. I actually made the back page of the *Guardian* the day after because they had taken a photograph of the protest.

The strangest thing I saw at Knowsley Road was when we played Warrington one year. We'd only been playing a few minutes and part of the roof from the stand fell off and nearly hit the touch judge. They cancelled the game and gave out vouchers to everyone so they could attend the replay free of charge.

I'll be sad to leave the ground for the last time. It's only when you're stood on the ground and certain memories come back to you like "remember that try?" and so on.

I think it will be very hard to recreate the atmosphere of Knowsley Road in the new stadium. One good thing about Knowsley Road that I like is that you're free to move anywhere around it.

The one thing I'd take with me to the new stadium is the playing surface, it's superb. It's like a bowling green and one of the best surfaces in Rugby League. I really hope that they take the posts with them. As for myself, I'd like a piece of turf from the ground. I suppose the floodlights would make one hell of a security light system for my house.

Mike

Mike has been a Saints supporter all his life and started watching the team regularly from 1985.

One early game that stands out for me is 1983 when Featherstone beat us in the Cup at home. There was loads of trouble behind the sticks. I was only young then and my dad put his coat round me because they were all kicking off all around us.

My first impression of the ground was the smell of the place. I used to love it. The smell of wintergreen. On a night game, when it was cold, you could see the steam rising off the pack. I mainly stood on the Popular side of the ground. That's where I prefer to stand because the atmosphere is very good there.

Kevin Ward is one of the Saints players who made their mark for me. Also, for his consistency Keiron Cunningham. He just does it week in and week out.

From the opposition, you have to say Ellery Hanley. He is by far the greatest player that I have ever seen. You've also got to look at the likes of Shaun Edwards, Andy Gregory and Andy Platt.

As for games that stand out for me at Knowsley Road, I have to say that the match against Bradford in the play-offs of 2000 was unbelievable. To score like that, well it was a miracle. Obviously the Wigan games are special. The day we won the Super League against Warrington in 1996 was a great day.

I'd say one of the best atmospheres at Saints was when Wigan beat us here 5-4 in the Lancashire Cup final in 1992. The defence was tremendous. It was so close, only a drop goal separated the sides. Anything could have happened near the end of the game. The ground was packed and even though no tries were scored, the atmosphere was electric.

The strangest thing I ever saw at Knowsley Road was when they had Sally Gunnell, the Olympic hurdler, as a guest at a Super League match in 1998. She did a hurdle race with St Bernard over some benches. God knows how much it cost to get her there. She didn't even know what type of rugby it was or anything.

In a way, I'll feel sad when we leave the ground for the last time. I'm disappointed that we are going because there is a lot of history there. Years ago, they could have turned that place around. They could have built it up. You can't replace the history and the heritage that they have there.

I think the thing I'll miss most is the fact that on Knowsley Road, wherever you are, you always feel close to the players. You always get the atmosphere. I'd say it's the best ground in terms of playing area and also viewing wise. The other good thing is that it's quite close to the Black Bull which is handy!

I won't miss the electronic scoreboard because, let's face it, it's never worked properly from day one, especially when it rains. I think they should take the posts from Knowsley Road to the new ground, at least you're taking some part of the history with you.

I'm going to try and get some souvenirs if possible and build myself a little Knowsley Road in my back garden!

I remember at the end of games, they used to let everyone run on the pitch and congratulate the players. It would be great for the little ones to do that again because some will have never experienced it. If you've never done it, you don't know what you're missing. It adds to the atmosphere to be able to run on the pitch at the end of the game and congratulate your team and ask for sock tie-ups and such as a kid.

And finally... Andrew Quirke

Here Andrew Quirke gives his recollections from his 21 years spent watching Saints. As well as commentating for visually-impaired supporters for a spell at the ground, he wrote and published Saints fanzines for 7 years and was also the publisher of an independent Saints website...

The first game that I can remember going to Knowsley Road to watch was actually when I was 3 years old. It was 1980 and we were playing the New Zealand touring side. I don't really remember much about the game except that I was freezing cold (winter rugby in those days) and that I was very impressed with the Haka that the New Zealand side had performed before the game. We won 11-6 which just goes to show how Rugby League internationals has changed over the years with the balance of power increasingly residing in Antipodean surroundings. That game was 21 years ago and I've been watching Saints ever since.

I got used to life at Knowsley Road very quickly. I would be taken to every home match from that young age and rarely missed a game at the ground. As soon as I was old enough I started going to some of the away games with my friends. I was brought up with Rugby League, surrounded by it and loved it. I used to be lifted over the turnstiles, as juniors used to do in those days, and plonked on the paddock wall every other Sunday. While sat on the perimeter wall, a steward would come past and tell me and other kids to keep our legs off the playing side of the wall. So we'd swing our legs back over, but as soon as the steward walked further down, we'd swing our legs back onto the playing side of the wall. The stewards were doing this for our own safety although we didn't see it like that at the time. If a player had run into us, we would have known about it and the wall wasn't that far away from the touchline. The problem was if you didn't have your legs over the wall you were far more uncomfortable. Sitting on the paddock wall was not comfortable and, to be honest, your bum went numb after a while. Of course, after an hour of this, I would start getting restless and annoy the people around me by constantly asking: "How long is there left?" I wasn't as bad as some of the kids you see at Saints games today though. You can see them all at the Edington end playing tick or hide and seek.

Another thing I recall is the people who used to wait outside the ground until half-time when they could get in for free.

My favourite player in my early days as a supporter was definitely Neil Holding. A very quick scrum-half with a good kicking game. He was like Bobbie Goulding in later years, a real character. In '96 Goulding helped us to the double and played a huge role in delivering that priceless feeling of success. As for Neil Holding, after finishing his career, he came back to Saints as the on-pitch announcer. He was excellent in this role and highly amusing, it was a shame that he left the club because he really added something to match days at Knowsley Road. He was also groundsman for a spell, helping Saints attain what is commonly acknowledged as the best playing surface in Rugby League. The two roles combined one Sunday when after receiving some stick from the visiting Warrington supporters he turned round, pointed to the surface and shouted: "You've never seen this at your place, this is grass," referring to the shocking state of the Wilderspool playing area at the time. I remember one night game in March 1984 I went to, as a young lad, against Hull that was later screened on *Scrumdown*, the ITV Rugby League programme of the eighties. Neil scored two fantastic tries to help us win the game. That was a great night, under the floodlights, with a big crowd because Hull were one of the teams to beat in the mid-eighties. There is always something special about night games I feel. Being in the Paddock, near to the pitch, you would not only get a pungent blast of liniment but you could hear the crunch of each tackle and see the steam rising off the players into the cold, night air. You could hear what the players were shouting at times, which meant a lot of young kids learnt a few words to show off in the playground. Some of the banter that went on between people in the paddock and some of the players was quite interesting as well, I remember one old fella shouted to a grinning Henderson Gill: "You've done more fouls than I've had hot dinners" - no bad language, nothing nasty.

The paddock would be made up of the same people every week. You'd have the kids on the wall at the front, parents standing behind them. Then you'd get the old men standing towards the back, with their shouts of "feeding" at every opposition scrum. You never used to see many women or girls at Saints games when I was a kid. One thing I do remember was that the Paddock never used to put up with any swearing. Obviously they didn't have to worry about me, not at that age anyway. If away fans came near the paddock and used a bit of colourful language they would be told to shut up or move on. The only expletive that was deemed acceptable was the occasional "bloody hell's fire Saints" when things weren't going to plan which in those days happened quite a lot.

I'd missed the 1976 Challenge Cup Final success against Widnes due to the small matter of being born a few months later. I'd also missed the glory years of the 1970s. We were never the worst team in the league in the 1980s but, as I remember, we were never the best either. It's not like today where we expect Saints to win every home game, a few teams in those days used to leave Knowsley Road with the two points. It was really a lean period in the 1980s but what it meant to me was when we did win and pull off a shock against a more fancied side, it meant that bit more to you. In these days of almost expecting a domestic trophy per season with only two to play for, it's totally different to those days of playing for the Lancashire

Cup, John Player Trophy, Challenge Cup, League title and Premiership, yet more often than not coming away empty handed.

I think my most disappointing afternoon as a Saints fan in those early years at least, and it still sends a shiver down my spine all of 18 years later, was the cup tie at home to Featherstone in 1983. It was a Saturday afternoon match screened on *Grandstand* and not only were we expected to win, we were expected to go onto Wembley. Featherstone were the total underdogs. Of course, they beat us with John Gilbert scoring two tries. I was heartbroken that day. Fev went onto upset Hull at Wembley and lift the Challenge Cup. That made it worse because we were thinking that could have been us. It's like "what might have been" and "there's always next year", all eternal cries of the second-placed team.

Mal Meninga

Then in 1984-85 there was Mal. *Vive la difference*. It had been reported in the papers all summer long that Saints were going to sign the Aussie centre Mal Meninga on a short-term deal. It got everyone in the town talking but most people were of the opinion that it was just paper talk and that Meninga would turn out to be nothing more than one of Saints' infamous irons in the fire. I was only seven but even I knew that Meninga would be a tremendous signing for the club. I did the unthinkable; I let Saints build my hopes up and thought he was going to come. As luck would have it, he did and the rest is history and an unforgettable signing. It was a ray of sunshine in an otherwise mostly overcast 1980s for the club. You might as well call that season 'the Meninga season'. I remember his debut. It was at home to Castleford who were a bit of a bogey side for us at the time. Mal scored two tries, made two tries and we won. He had an instant impact. We won the Lancashire Cup and Premiership Trophy. In fact, on the way to winning the Premiership, we destroyed Wigan at home in front of 18,000 just days after their classic Wembley encounter with Hull. That was Mal's last game at Knowsley Road for Saints. The one dark spot on the season was a night match in the Challenge Cup preliminary round against Hull

174

KR. Again, we were expected to get to Wembley. Saints were well and truly riding on the crest of the Meninga wave. We had other good players in the side as well that season including a lot of local lads like Holding and skipper Harry Pinner. Meninga played stand-off that night and he tried everything he knew but we got beaten and our Wembley dream was shattered again with the pessimistic realisation that "if we can't get to Wembley with Meninga, what chance have we got without him?". You can't over-emphasise Mal's contribution to the team even though during some matches he would be subbed at half-time such was our dominance over the opposition. Mal scored 28 tries that season and made a lot more. We didn't win the league that year but it was a season of great memories nonetheless. My abiding memory of Mal for some reason is one night match where we were winning comfortably and Mal was putting some big tackles in. One old man who had been there through thick and thin for many years had a big smile on his face and was shouting: "Come to daddy" with glee.

After that memorable season, Mal was constantly linked with a move back to the club but it never happened. It might be for the best as our memories remained safely unbroken of this Aussie legend. Anyone who has met Mal off the pitch will tell you he is a total ambassador for Rugby League. He only played a handful of games for Saints but he will never be forgotten and who knows, one day he could be Saints coach? That 1984-85 season lifted the entire town.

The Scaff

Later as a teenager, the place I used to stand was commonly known as the Scaff. To all of you who do not know of the Scaff, it's the halfway line underneath the television gantry. This is where all the young boys and girls gather and chant various nice, clean songs at the opposition. The best description I've heard of this particular sweat box is that it's the engine room of the crowd. Certainly, it has an atmosphere all of it's own. If you were standing there for the big games like Wigan, you'd have to be prepared for being moved along several yards when there was a try. It was noisy, hot, sweaty and, at good moments for Saints, clinically insane. The main job for the Scaff is, of course, to get the singing going and create a good atmosphere.

The game I remember there most is the day after Boxing Day in 1992, the derby against Wigan. This was when Wigan were at their best. They had Platt, Skerrett, Clarke, Offiah, Edwards; the list went on and on. They were the only full-time pros while everyone else was part-time. Everyone else in the league was struggling just to get near Wigan let alone overtake them but it wasn't a level playing field. It hurt Saints more than anyone though being in Wigan's shadow. We were their closest and deadliest rivals and it was sickening watching them lift trophy after trophy while we were starved of success. I remember this game vividly. Saints wore a one-off Coors sponsored jersey for the game and after it plenty of supporters thought they should wear it every week. I was standing with all my mates directly under the gantry where Eddie and Stevo were commentating for Sky TV. We had got there hours before the match to start the singing. In fact, by the time the game started, our voices were nearly gone. No one had given Saints a chance in this game. Wigan scored first and Botica kicked the conversion from the touchline. It was 6-0 and we all thought "same old story". Unbelievably, that was the last time Wigan scored all day. Saints totally destroyed them and it ended up 41-6. I remember being stood underneath the TV gantry after one try and looking up seeing some of my mates actually standing on it celebrating wildly. The team was a mix of local lads like Gary Connolly with overseas players like Tea Ropati. Any victory over Wigan though is memorable, it's just the nature of those games isn't it? Like when we beat them 38-14 on Good Friday 2000 when we had players missing, it's always a bit special, especially on your home ground. A Saints - Wigan game has an atmosphere all of its own. The ground is packed, there is a lot of noise. Even days before the match, you're thinking about how Saints will go on and you're nervous so God knows what the actual players must be feeling. You ask yourself the question: "can they do it?" You hope against hope that they can. If you actually do win it lifts the whole town for weeks. The flip side is the negative feelings you have before the game like: "I hope we don't get hammered". They are actually very hard games to watch, almost unbearable at times because you're so tense and wrapped up in the game. So, as you can imagine winning them is totally off the chart in terms of sheer joy.

My other main memory of my time on the Scaff was Kevin Ward. Wardy was the hero of the Scaff without doubt; similar to Bobbie Goulding a few years later. A lot of people said that he was too old when we signed him but he's the best prop forward I've seen in a Saints' shirt bar none. He put in some great displays and it was a tragedy that his career was cut short by a horrific leg injury.

Another thing I recall about my time on the Scaff was a Wednesday night match against Castleford. There's always something about a night match that increases the atmosphere somehow and underneath the floodlights that night there was a really good atmosphere in the ground and Saints were playing really well. The Australians were over at the time for the test series as well as some games against some club sides. I got talking to this Aussie bloke who had come over to see as much Rugby League as he could. He had stood on the Scaff to get involved in the atmosphere, the singing and chanting that we take for granted, but that just doesn't happen as much in Australia. Well, he certainly got the atmosphere that night. The Scaff were on form and when Saints scored were going wild. This Aussie was only a little bloke and he was joining in with the exuberant celebrations as best as he could but was being moved about on this human tide of Saints' excitement. He really enjoyed the game and couldn't believe how involved the crowd got. I remember telling him: "we've got Wigan next week, if you think this is something, get a load of what it'll be like against them".

Commentary

In 1995, I used to do a bit of commentary for visually-impaired supporters at home games. They sit at the back of D stand where there are headphone sockets and we would give them full match commentary from the press box. So they could go to the game and soak up all the atmosphere, and we'd make sure they were up on play and knew what was going on. Basically, I'd get there a couple of hours before the game, go into Saints' quite tiny equipment room and get what I needed. Then you'd walk out through the tunnel onto the pitch. Obviously, it's every young local lad's dream to walk out through that tunnel as a Saints player and it must be an amazing feeling doing that. I mean, when you were playing Wigan and there's 15,000 there, walking through the tunnel must be amazing. They've changed where they come out now, the players dressing rooms are under the main stand and they come out from there but until the past couple of years, the teams came out through that narrow tunnel. Walking out of it, you can just see the Edington end of the ground and you see just what a great stadium Knowsley Road is. It's only when you're standing on the pitch that you realise how big and wide the playing area is.

So, I'd walk across the pitch, to the main stand and go up to the press box. Then I'd set everything up and test that all the equipment was working. We would start off at about quarter to three, we'd have the team sheets by then so we'd go through the selections. We would give a match preview running through the form of the opposition and any Saints news we might have heard. Then we'd do full match commentary. Sometimes we'd get the odd guest joining us like an injured or past Saints player. The hardest thing I found was when we played teams like Workington and it was a nightmare trying to identify the players because you didn't know who they were.

The first game I commentated on was during the Centenary season on the 5 November 1995, against Halifax. Saints won very convincingly that day. I was very nervous at first but it's surprising how quickly you get used to it. I really enjoyed it, but talking about Rugby League is something I have a lot of practice at anyway.

There are a number of games I commentated on that stand out for me. The first is the Regal Trophy semi-final against Warrington in 1995 when we won 80-0. Everyone was expecting the game to be a really close semi-final, a typical derby match. Saints just ripped them apart. Bobbie Goulding was on song, the team was firing on all cylinders and it was a fantastic display. Perelini had a good game that night but got injured and was supposed to come off. The supporters were applauding him as he walked to the bench. He decided he wanted to carry on and limped back into the action. I remember the end of the game and I was commentating with the guy who ran the commentary service. I was talking when the Saints players were applauding the supporters on the main stand side where I was at the top in the press box. I actually put the microphone down, which is a cardinal sin in commentary, leaving silence or dead air for a while, and I started applauding the side after such a good display. I couldn't help it really, the Saints speccie in me took over. I don't think it went down too well with my co-commentator but it was a spur-of-the-moment thing.

One other little problem that troubled us was that the view from the press box was far from perfect, just as it is for everyone in the stand. The view is obstructed by the left-hand side of the stand where it finishes and so if anything important is happening in the corner you've got to hope they move the ball back towards the posts quickly.

I remember one game that Saints played and me and my co-commentator Mike were really having a go at Danny Arnold in the first half. At half-time, a gentleman who accompanied the visually-impaired supporters at Saints informed us that Danny Arnold's mum was listening to the commentary. In the second half, we did a complete about-face and praised him to the highest heavens.

The next game that stands out for me was a game against Workington in 1995. That may sound like a strange choice but it was Paul Newlove's debut. We'd signed him the week before for a world record fee of £500,000 with £250,000 of that being made up by Bernard Dwyer, Paul Loughlin and Sonny Nickle leaving the club. That was a shame because they had all been good servants to the club but there was a lot of anticipation over Newlove's debut. He looked a class act and had been prolific as a try scorer for Featherstone and Bradford. At the time, he was being described as the final piece in the Saints puzzle. I remember it was a really wet day with Saints winning convincingly. I have to admit that my eyesight isn't the best and sitting at the back of the stand when there's driving rain makes identifying players even harder. Danny

Arnold, it could be argued, looks a bit like Newlove from a distance. Well, that's my story anyway. Danny picked that day to have a blinder. He scored three tries but each time he scored I confidently announced: "And there's Paul Newlove with his first try for Saints" only to be corrected by my co-commentator. Right at the end of the game though, Newy did score. He broke through and actually fell over with no one near him, but because it was wet he slid over. Not his best try for Saints but the first of many. After the game, I'd have to take the commentary equipment back to Saints' equipment room. On the way to nicking a butty or two from the buffet, you'd see coaches and players giving interviews outside the dressing rooms. I've seen a couple of good arguments down there after matches. I also had the chance to speak to the likes of Harry Cook who was always given a standing ovation when announced to the banqueting suite before a game. I did the commentary job for a couple of years and it was really interesting. You see different sides of the sport through it. You get a look at what happens behind the scenes before and after the game. You see the game itself in a slightly different way as well. You're still a Saints fan but you have to try and look at it as neutrally as possible as well as concentrating on getting the players' names right. In the press box, and I imagine, the restaurant and executive boxes, you do get the atmosphere of the game but partly feel sealed away from the action. There is always that glass barrier between you and what's going on like you're watching it on television.

New Era

One game that particularly sticks in the memory was the penultimate game of the 1996 Super League season. All season, we had blasted our opposition under excellent coach Shaun McRae, with stars such as Scott Gibbs, Paul Newlove, Bobbie Goulding, Apollo Perelini and Karle Hammond leading the way.

This game was against Sheffield, it was a Sunday night match live on Sky TV with a noisy crowd and a very special atmosphere. We were zeroing in on the double after our long-awaited Wembley triumph earlier in the year. The feeling we shared was that we thought we were going to do it but we also knew if Saints lost one game Wigan would win the title. Saints being Saints, it was always possible we could lose a silly game. Saints are unpredictable if nothing else and this led to a lot of nervous moments during the run-in. Would we fall at the final hurdle? We had not won the league title for so many years and wanted it desperately. That Sunday night though, if ever a team was on fire, this was it. We totally hammered Sheffield 68-2, it was as complete a performance from a side as you are likely to see. Everyone in the crowd was singing, it was great. In fact, the crowd were so happy with what they were seeing that when mascot St Bernard picked up the ball at half-time and scored a try, which Sky then replayed on the big screen, everyone went bananas. Steve Prescott scored four tries that night and the fourth was one of the best tries I have seen at the ground. Goulding and Sullivan combined to send in Prescott who collected the ball with a spectacular dive as it bounced over the opposition line - sensational stuff and a real Saints try if ever there was one. The Sunday after, the championship decider against Warrington wasn't as good in some ways as that game against Sheffield although in other ways, of course, it was better. I was standing on the Scaff for both games and they were both something special. That night against Sheffield, I think we all realised that we weren't going to be denied, that we were the best team and that we were going to be crowned champions. All those final defeats, all the heartbreak of the years gone by, wiped out by the fantastic double we achieved in 1996.

Of course, we gave Warrington a good hiding to clinch the title. There was an 18,000 plus crowd at Knowsley Road which was tremendous to be part of. Many of the crowd had made tin foil trophies or brought banners. After the game, the team did the lap of honour with the Challenge Cup and the Super League trophy and it was unbelievable. The moment that Bobbie Goulding lifted the Super League trophy in front of a packed halfway line populace was a defining moment. No longer were we the bridesmaids, finally we had done it and jumped out of the shadows into the spotlight that only champions enjoy. I think another defining moment that helped bring us to that point was an off-the-field occurrence at Knowsley Road. It was before Super League began and newly appointed chief executive of the club David Howes invited fans to ask him questions in an open meeting. He outlined his vision and ambitions for the club and made it clear that we weren't going to be also-rans. As part of the throng there in that overcrowded room at Saints, little did I realise that his appointment was the start of something big for the club after so many false dawns. He, along with Shaun McRae, installed a new professionalism into the club and they were both popular with supporters. The success they helped us to was amazing. Lifting the league title on your own ground in front of your home fans is something a little bit special. After the long, dark winter of Wigan's dominance it was fitting that this was our time in the sun in the new summer era of Super League.

Knocking Wigan out of the Cup

Another game I'd pick is one I commentated on, the unforgettable game against Wigan in February 1997 in the Challenge Cup. The previous year they'd been knocked out of the Cup for the first time in years by Salford in a huge upset. Everyone was expecting Wigan to get straight back to Wembley though.

They had a full-strength team against us but they did have several players returning from playing Rugby Union in the winter and no one knew how that was going to affect them. They were red-hot favourites. We were used to them knocking us out of competitions left, right and centre during their decade of success. We started really well and looked quite good. Just before half-time though, Bobbie Goulding did a high tackle on Neil Cowie. Bobbie got sent off and I remember thinking: "that's it, game over, 12 men against Wigan for 40 minutes, there's no chance" but I had to try and put across to the listeners that the game was still on and Saints could still do it. It was hard though and to be honest I felt gutted at half-time. When I came down from the press box at half-time all the Wigan fans were totally delighted. The Saints fans were all saying: "We've done it again, thrown it away".

However, in the second half there was only one team in it and that was Saints. It was probably the best second 40 minutes I've seen from Saints at Knowsley Road. We had one man less against one hell of a good team. It wasn't just any man we were missing though, it was our playmaker and inspiration, Mr Goulding. The likes of Karle Hammond, Paul Newlove, Chris Joynt and Derek McVey all worked really hard for each other and we ended up winning 26-12. The best moment was when Alan Hunte intercepted a Henry Paul pass and it clinched us the game. I was trying to stay calm as Hunte was racing away because I was doing the commentary. Inside though, I knew this was the moment we had been awaiting a long time. Knocking Wigan out of the cup after all their success. It was an amazing moment. I don't think I'll ever forget that day.

The scoreboard end

I had a spell of standing at the scoreboard end which is usually packed with Saints fans but it's very much out in the open. So if the weather is inclement, it's not a good place to stand. However, it was where I was standing the night an unforgettable try was scored. I am, of course, talking about Saints play-off game against Bradford in September 2000 when time was up and we were trailing by a point and all hope was lost. Nine passes and a kick later, one of the most spectacular tries I have ever seen, and the most dramatic ending to a game in memory saw Saints win against all odds. That Chris Joynt try is definitely the most unforgettable try at the ground, for me even beating Les Quirk's late length-of-the-field effort against Hull in February 1991. It was typical Saints, thrilling, keeping the ball alive at all costs and totally unexpected. The ground erupted as Joynt went over and it was just mayhem, extraordinary stuff. Everyone went wild, it was incredible, a miracle try. I still get wound up watching it on video some time after the event, listening to the commentators, you can hear the excitement in their voices: "It's wide to West, inside to Joynt". Joynty will always be remembered for that try and I'm glad because he's been a class skipper for Saints. He always seems to do it in the big games for us, scoring two tries in our Grand

Final win over Wigan in 2000. Then there was his crucial try in the World Club Championship against Brisbane and scoring against Wigan at Knowsley Road in February 2001 to help knock the pie-eaters out of the Challenge Cup.

For the past couple of years, I have watched the game at the Edington end of the ground. That's where the away supporters tend to congregate so it goes without saying that I never stand there when Wigan are playing. You have a good laugh there especially with some of the Yorkshire speccies, particularly when Saints are giving them a good hiding. It has quite a good atmosphere as well because Rugby League is one sport where you can mix with the away fans. It's a cliché but it's not a lie that Rugby League is a family sport. You rarely see bother at Rugby League games anymore. You can talk to away fans in the pub before and after the game with no problems. It's not just going to the ground through the turnstiles that's part of the game-day experience, it's also peoples' varying pre-match rituals. Whether it's going down to the Black Bull, Triplex club or Bird I'th Hand for a pre-match pint and talking about the game to come. Then you go to the spot where you stand every game and nine times out of ten, it's the same people standing with you and around you each time.

In recent years I used to sell copies of my Saints fanzine at the ground. It was nice going round selling copies and people making good comments about liking something you've published.

The strangest thing I've ever seen there was a cold winter's night during the close season one year when a radio station put on a laser display and firework show. Standing on the terraces, glad to be back on the ground, you could see all manner of laser shapes on the pitch. It was a surreal experience.

Players

I've been lucky enough to see the Aussie touring sides play here in 1982, 1986, 1990 and 1994. You tend to watch them with simple awe. You never go to those games thinking that Saints could cause an upset. You just go and watch it and admire how good the Aussie sides are. It's like the World Club Challenge in 1997 where every British team got hammered. The thing was though it was good to see the likes of Stacey Jones and Mat Rogers in this country. These are modern-day greats and in years to come people will possibly be talking about some of those players as legends. It was good to see that calibre of world class player on the famous Knowsley Road turf.

As for the imports I've seen at Saints, there's been a lot and to be truthful they've been a mixed bag.

I thought Paul Vautin tried really hard at Saints while his compatriot Michael O'Connor was a big disappointment. Derek McVey had a couple of good years at Saints and helped to provide us with some success because he could offload in the tackle. That was something we had lacked since the great Kevin Ward. Shane Cooper was another one, he was the captain for a few years, and was an excellent playmaker and tactician. He gave his all for Saints and, like one of my mates always says, he got away with murder when the ref wasn't looking. He would give a crafty dig to a player off the ball and never get caught. Phil Veivers was also a loyal servant.

We've had so much home-grown talent at Knowsley Road, we've been blessed with so many over the years. Two of the best I've seen are two we've got at the moment. One is Keiron Cunningham who is the best hooker in the world. The other one is Paul Wellens and he's got so much potential that it's scary.

Of the opposition players who stand out, obviously you have to mention the likes of Ellery Hanley. He stands out not just as the captain of that all-conquering Wigan side but also as coach of Saints. One of my main memories of 1999 was, after we had beaten Castleford to earn our place in the Grand Final, Ellery striding onto the pitch to a great ovation. He gave a speech to the Saints fans saying we were going to get "stronger and stronger". He announced the signings of Cunningham and Long on new contracts. Ellery had a special affinity and bond with the Saints fans at that time. It was during that game that the newly re-signed Long beat five Castleford players to score a magnificent individual try.

That brings me to the demonstration the fans had for Hanley earlier in the 1999 season. We played Hull and beat them easily but it's one of the only times I've been to Knowsley Road and no one really gave a monkey's about the game. People were fed up with what had been happening at the club. He had been suspended and a rumour was going round that he was going to be sacked. I've never experienced an atmosphere quite like it. There were chants of "Ellery, Ellery" throughout the game. At the end of the game, there were about 2,000 fans I think that stayed on the ground for about an hour. There was a sit down protest and it showed the depth of feeling at the time. The fans had decided to put their point across and it showed they weren't just going to accept things.

Hanley was definitely one of the greatest opposition players I've seen at Knowsley Road.

I have to say also, that although I never liked the bloke, Shaun Edwards was a tremendous player as well.

Recent times

When we won the title again after crushing the old enemy Wigan at Old Trafford in October 2000, the club held a fan appreciation day at Knowsley Road. The team did a lap of honour with the Super League trophy in front of more than 10,000 fans. This also included the strange sight of Freddie Tuilagi and Apollo Perelini doing a Samoan dance around the pitch. They were joined by a clearly inebriated Sean Long who stripped down to his thong - not something you see every week at the ground! To be the champions at the end of one century and millennium is one thing and to start a new century as champions, World Club champions and Challenge Cup winners after the fantastic Brisbane and Bradford wins is another. To complete the treble with a clean sweep of trophies is a magnificent achievement for Ian Millward's men. It will ensure that the current side will be talked about for years to come as not only one of the greatest ever Saints sides, but one of the greatest Rugby League sides, because in the full-time era they have won an incredible seven trophies in six years.

The typical Super League game for Saints sees fans turning up expecting the side to win. When I look back to how it used to be, it's amazing really how things have changed. There are young kids today who have seen us win trophy after trophy and as far as they know it's never been any different. Now it's: "How many are we going to win by today?" When I started going it was: "Are we going to win at all?" A lot of the time in Super League, we tend to run away with games in the second half, often scoring 40 or 50 points. We've always been an entertaining team. No matter who's come and gone, what players or coaches we've had, we've always scored tries and always will. We've always played with a certain spirit that sees us throw the ball. You'll never take the flair away from Saints. I know we'll take that to the new stadium with us. My main memory of Knowsley Road is the type of rugby we have played since we have been there. The unpredictability and excitement of watching Saints and the atmosphere in the crowd especially on big occasions. As for souvenirs from the ground, I'd have to say some of the famous turf of course and one of the current corner flags at the ground because I sponsor them!

When I leave the ground for the last time, I think it's going to be very strange. In a way people aren't really going to be able to believe it. At the end of the last home game, people are going to be walking off quite slowly. It's going to be very hard for people who've been watching rugby there for 40 or 50 years or more. It's going to be a sad occasion tempered by the fact that hopefully the move will give Saints more financial security. It's a special place to all of us and we've all spent a lot of time there. People have grown up there on the terraces from generation to generation. The place has a unique atmosphere and ambience all of its own. It will live on in people's memories and we all have our part to play when we're grandparents. Then we will have to bore our grandkids with our tales of life at Knowsley Road while they find it hard to believe that people used to stand up at matches.

Leaving aside the fact that Knowsley Road is a Rugby League ground, it is also a very important building in the town's fabric. I know this because I can see the ground's floodlights from my bedroom window! When it goes an irreplaceable part of the St Helens' landscape will go with it. It is known throughout and beyond the town. The words "Knowsley Road" are familiar to Rugby League supporters all over the world. When the ground goes, a large chunk of the town's social history will go with it. St Helens is a town known for two things, Rugby League and glass. With the glass industry scaling down considerably, the Rugby League is all that is left and its home in the town for so long will be remembered by both the supporters and the wider community.

The move to a new stadium is on the horizon and as this book ends, a new chapter in the club's history is about to unfold. The new stadium should guarantee that magical nights like the one where Saints defeated Brisbane Broncos against all odds at the Reebok Stadium in Bolton to become World Club Champions in January 2001 will, in future, be able to take place in St Helens. If the new stadium can generate even a small amount of the passion and history that its predecessor did, then the club will go from strength to strength.

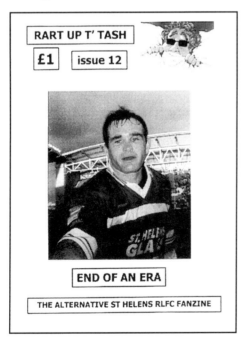

The final edition of Rart Up T'Tash, the Saints fanzine edited by Andrew Quirke. This was the end of an era of seven years of fanzine publishing. This edition was at the end of the 2000 season.

Appendices

1: Stadium Chronology

September 1890: First game played at the ground. The opposition was Manchester Rangers, a game which St Helens won. At the time, Knowsley Road was little more than a field with stewards taking admission fees at small holes in fencing at what is now the Edington end of the ground.

September 1895: The first Northern Union fixture at the ground, took place on 7 September 1895. Rochdale Hornets were the opposition and they were duly dispatched 8-3. The first points were scored by Saints captain Billy Cross with a drop goal.

Early 1900s: Original main stand built from public subscription. Demolished in late 1950s.

February 1909: The first Australian touring side came to St Helens and were beaten 9-0 despite having a live kangaroo as their mascot.

December 1920: Ground improvements included the addition of the pavilion which is the oldest surviving part of the ground. It was opened by Lord Derby in front of a 24,000 crowd for the visit of Wigan and included a gym, bath and offices. The ground and pavilion were later purchased from the Pilkington Brothers for £2,403.

December 1925: The popular side stand was opened at the Swinton home game. It was 100 feet long. Two years later, a further 125 feet was added at a total cost of £1,063 in order to cover the whole of the terracing on that side of the ground. The structure was then capable of holding 2,000 people. Fund-raising for the stand was began by Jesse Skepper, secretary and founder member of the Supporters Club.

War years 1939-1945: The ground contained an air-raid warden's post as well as provisions for using the dressing rooms as emergency clearing stations for casualties. Eventually, the pitch was attacked by nothing more ferocious than a farmer's cows who were allowed to graze on the hallowed turf.

January 1950: The training pitch was completed. 'The Allotments', the land on which it stood between the pavilion and Dunriding Lane, had been purchased by the club in 1930. Today, the training pitch is used for pre-match entertainment such as bouncy castles.

February 1951: The Edington stand, traditional haunt for away supporters, was opened against Bradford.

1955: The original scoreboard completed which later became the police control room, since demolished.

August 1958: The main stand as it is today, was opened by Sir Harry Pilkington. It had cost over £30,000 with room for over 2,000 seated supporters. It had been erected in a little over three months and had been paid for partly by local firms' donations while the rest was provided by the very successful Saints Supporters' Club. Steel for the new main stand was supplied by the Todd brothers. The stand overhung at the rear to avoid a railway line behind it. The former railway cutting was later filled in and was turned into a car park.

1961: A new popular side stand was added along with improved dressing room facilities. In September, one of the original wooden goalposts was blown down in freak gales. Metal posts replaced them until 1998 saw the need for moveable posts when Liverpool FC Reserves began playing at the ground, and international football stars such as Steve McManaman and Robbie Fowler have since trodden the Knowsley Road turf.

January 1965: New floodlights were switched on against an Other Nationalities team. They cost more than £10,000.

Early 1970s: The original club shop, very different from the Saints Superstore introduced in the 1990s, was opened.

March 1973: The bar and restaurant was opened by Lord Pilkington.

1989: The pavilion was extended to house a new sponsor's lounge. The right hand terrace was developed to make room for nine executive boxes. An electronic scoreboard was added, and a permanent TV gantry on halfway line of the popular side. Before this, camera crews used a less-than-sturdy scaffold. The crowd there are still known as 'The Scaff' and generate much of the ground's atmosphere and noise.

Mid 1990s: New dressing rooms and a gym were also built under the main stand. Before then, the teams came out from the players' tunnel at the clubhouse end of the ground. A pop video was filmed at Knowsley Road in 1995 as ex-Crowded House members the Finn brothers turned up to see Saints play Castleford in the centenary season. The black and white video *Suffer Never* saw the Finn brothers watching the game, clips of the action and then follows Sonny Nickle down the tunnel. The video was shown on satellite channel VH-1.

Late 1990s: The scaffolding necessary for the Sky TV video screen was permanently erected for televised games. This was situated at the far corner of the clubhouse end to the left of the scoreboard.

1999: Knowsley Road was used to recreate Old Trafford in the 1960s for filming *Best*, the story of footballer George Best. Stars Patsy Kensit and Liam Gallagher (who was not actually in the film) came to the ground.

Summer 2000: Plans to move to a new stadium and the sale of Knowsley Road to housing developers are announced.

2: Club honours

World Club Championship: Winners: 2001.
Runners-up: 1976, 2000
Super League Grand Final: Winners: 1999, 2000
Super League Europe Champions: 1996
Rugby League Championship:
Winners: 1931-32, 1952-53, 1958-59, 1969-70, 1970-71
Runners-up: 1964-65, 1966-67, 1971-72
Division 1:Champions 1974-75
Runners-up: 1962-63, 1973-74, 1976-77, 1984-85, 1986-87, 1987-88, 1991-92, 1992-93
League Leaders Trophy: Winners 1964-65, 1965-66
Club Championship (merit table) : Runners-up: 1973-74
Challenge Cup: Winners: 1955-56, 1960-61, 1965-66, 1971-72, 1975-76, 1996, 1997, 2001
Runners-up: 1896-97, 1914-15, 1929-30, 1952-53, 1977-78, 1986-87, 1988-89, 1990-91
Lancashire Cup: Winners: 1926-27, 1953-54, 1960-61, 1961-62, 1962-63, 1963-64, 1964-65, 1967-68, 1968-69, 1984-85, 1991-92
Runners-up: 1932-33, 1952-53, 1956-57, 1958-59, 1959-60, 1970-71, 1982-83, 1992-93
John Player Trophy: Winners 1987-88
Lancashire League: Winners 1929-30, 1931-32, 1952-53, 1959-60, 1964-65, 1965-66, 1966-67, 1968-69
Premiership Trophy: Winners: 1975-76, 1976-77, 1984-85, 1992-93
Runners-up:1974-75, 1987-88, 1991-92, 1996, 1997
Western Division: Champions 1963-64
BBC Trophy: Winners 1971-72, 1975-76
Runners-up: 1965-66, 1968-69, 1970-71, 1977-78, 1978-79
CIS Charity Shield : Winners 1992-93

Match records

Goals in a match: 16 by Paul Loughlin versus Carlisle, 14 September 1986
Tries in a match: 6
Alf Ellaby versus Barrow, 5 March 1932
Steve Llewellyn versus Castleford, 3 March 1956
Steve Llewellyn versus Liverpool City, 20 August 1956
Tom van Vollenhoven versus Wakefield Trinity, 21 December 1957
Tom van Vollenhoven versus Blackpool Borough, 23 April 1962
Frank Myler versus Maryport, 1 Sept 1969
Shane Cooper versus Hull, 7 February 1988
Points in a match: 40 Paul Loughlin versus Carlisle, 14 September 1986
Highest Score: 112-0 versus Carlisle 14 Sept 1986
Highest Against: 65-12 versus Wigan 26 May 1997
Highest Attendance: 35,695 versus Wigan 26 Dec 1949

Season records

Goals: 214 by Kel Coslett, 1971-72
Tries: 62 by Tom Van Vollenhoven, 1958-59
Points: 452 by Kel Coslett, 1971-72

Career records

Goals: 1,639 by Kel Coslett, 1961-1976
Tries: 392 by Tom van Vollenhoven, 1957-1968
Points: 3,413 by Kel Coslett, 1961-1976
Appearances: 519+12 subs by Kel Coslett, 1961-1976

Bibliography

Saints in their Glory - Alex Service 1985
March of the Saints - Alex Service 1988
Marching On (A celebration of St Helens RLFC at the Millennium) - Alex Service and Denis Whittle 1999

TWO GREAT RUGBY LEAGUE BOOKS
FROM THE PARRS WOOD PRESS

One Winter - Romance, Rock 'n' Roll and Rugby League in the Swinging Sixties

Set in the fictional town of Ashurst in south Lancashire in the early sixties, against the background of one of the worst winters in living memory and the great St Helens team of the same period, *One Winter* is a vivid and humorous account of working class life at home, work and play.

"... a lovingly produced novel... One Winter is a book about people, and the bonds they forge with one another to get them through their daily struggle...Through his book, Lee appears to be hankering for a time when a sense of community reigned supreme, both in Rugby League... and in the wider society which the game is used as a very coherent symbol for."

TONY HANNAN, Total League

PAPERBACK - 192 PAGES - ISBN: 1 903158 01 X - £7.99

The Cup - Passion, Murder and a Quest for a Sporting Grail

It is the end of the nineteenth century. The world is changing and as it changes, Chorley and Lancashire change with it.

As his own life unravels before him, Humphrey Whittle can only reflect on an earlier time, a time of heroes, when Chorley Rugby Football Club swept all before them in the first rugby football knockout cup. A time when Humphrey was captain of the team, a young man starting out in a life of business and politics, one desperate to win the affections of a cruel father and conquer the fear of madness and failure that haunts him.

Humphrey Whittle's entire life has been shaped by the Quest for The Cup. But twenty years after Chorley's season of glory, Humphrey is faced with a terrible choice, a choice that will have grave consquences for the one he loves...

PAPERBACK - 232 PAGES - ISBN: 1 903158 20 6 - £8.95

Both books available from all good bookshops or by mail order at the cover prices
POST FREE (UK only) from:
The Parrs Wood Press, FREEPOST, Manchester M15 9PW
CREDIT CARD ORDERS AND TRADE ENQUIRIES: 0161-226-4466 OR sport@parrswoodpress.com
www.parrswoodpress.com

194

Rugby League Analysis, History & Vision

If you want to read about Rugby League in depth,
this is the magazine for you.

Published twice a year, it concentrates on the history of the game, and
analysis of current issues facing the game. It has a lively book review
section and a regular obituary section. Leading Rugby League writers
contribute regularly, including Robert Gate, Harry Edgar, Michael O'Hare,
Huw Richards and Phil Melling.

Order the latest issue for £2.00, or subscribe:

£7.00 for 4 issues   or

£10.00 for three issues plus a copy of one of the following books:
Tries in the Valleys - A history of Rugby League in Wales
From Fulham to Wembley - 20 years of Rugby League in London
The Fulham Dream - Rugby League comes to London

Order form: (Photocopy if you do not want to cut the book)
(Tick box)
Please send me the latest issue for £2.00   []
I would like a subscription:
£7.00 for 4 issues   []   £10.00 for 3 issues plus a book   []
Book chosen:

Name:

Address:

Phone:

Please send to: London League Publications Ltd, PO Box 10441, London E14 0SB.
Cheques payable to London League Publications Ltd, no credit cards.

Rugby League books from London League Publications

Rugby's Class War
Bans, boot money and parliamentary battles
by David Hinchliffe M.P.
The story of League's battles with Union in parliament.
Published in November 2000 at £9.75. Special offer £9.00

From Fulham to Wembley
20 years of Rugby League in London
Edited by Dave Farrar and Peter Lush
A celebration of 20 years of professional rugby league in the capital.
Published in May 2000 at £8.75 Special offer £8.00

The Fulham Dream
Rugby League comes to London
by Harold Genders
The inside story of the creation of Fulham RLFC and the promotion
winning first season.
Published in September 2000 at £6.95. Special offer £6.00

London books special offer: **The above two titles for £12.00.**

The Rugby League Grounds Guide
By Peter Lush and Dave Farrar
Published in April 2001 at £7.95. Special offer £7.00

Tries in the Valleys
A History of Rugby League in Wales
Edited by Peter Lush and Dave Farrar
Published in 1997 at £14.95. Special offer £8.00

All orders post free in UK, £1 per book overseas.
Order from: London League Publications Ltd., PO Box 10441,
London E14 0SB.
Cheques payable to London League Publications Ltd, no credit card orders.